BEHAVIORAL SCIENCE
FOR THE BOREDS

by Frederick S. Sierles, M.D.

Professor and Director,
Medical Student Education in
Psychiatry and Behavioral Science
University of Health Sciences/The Chicago Medical School,
and
Fellow, American Psychiatric Association

MedMaster, Inc., Miami

ISBN # 0-940780-11-9

Made in the United States of America

Published by
MedMaster, Inc.
P.O. Box 640028
Miami, FL 33164

to Hannah and Joshua

Other books by the author:

Sierles, F.S., ed.: *Clinical Behavioral Science,* SP Medical and Scientific Books, Jamaica, NY (1982).
Taylor, M.A., Sierles, F.S., and Abrams, R.: *General Hospital Psychiatry,* Free Press, New York (1985).

CONTENTS

PREFACE

I wrote this book to help you get a good score on the Behavioral Science section of Part I of the National Boards. This could free some of your time and your instructors' time for more creative educational efforts in behavioral science and psychiatry. Also, some of the material may be useful for your future practice of medicine, but this was not my main purpose in writing the book.

I thank Dolores Turowski for her typing, Laurene Sierles for her indexing, Stephen Goldberg for his familiarity with medical student culture, Marshall Falk and Michael Alan Taylor for their encouragement, Mary Lou Liebert and Joyce Olivares for helping with the final drafts, Marlene Weber-Shea for her illustrations, and Frank Naeymi-Rad for producing the computer disc, V. Chowdary Jampala for explaining diagnostic sensitivity and specificity to me, and Michael Schrift for reviewing the chapter on behavioral neurochemistry.

Opinions expressed in this book are not necessarily those of the Chicago Medical School or of the American Psychiatric Association.

A word about the title: In addition to (hopefully) being "eye-catching" to students browsing in medical bookstores (I never took a vow of poverty.), it reflects the ambivalence that I and scores of colleagues and students feel about the National Board Examinations. On the one hand, they have rightly compelled medical schools to value behavior in their curricula. On the other, they have created a high-stakes guessing game about which topics and details they're going to stress each year, and which disciplinary boundaries they're going to cross.

For example, by only the most liberal definition (i.e., a behaviorally-related subject accessible to systematic study) can medical ethics be labelled a behavioral science. I doubt whether you, the reader, presume medical ethics to be the primary province of psychiatrists, psychologists, sociologists or other behavioral scientists. But as the joke goes, "It's a dirty job and somebody's got to do it."

My attitude towards the behavioral sciences is reverential. I became a practitioner, teacher and researcher in psychiatry to immerse myself in the study of behavior.

If you find this book useful, it will have served its purpose. If you find some of its content challenging, as I do, I will be overjoyed.

Chapter 1:

BIOSTATISTICS AND OTHER ASPECTS OF RESEARCH

I. STATISTICS AND PROBABILITY

Most medical research using statistics requires making correlations and comparisons. An example of a correlation is "What is the relationship between the number of times (if at all) a medical student cheated when he was in college, and the number of times he cheated in medical school?" An example of a comparison is "Among patients hospitalized for posttraumatic stress disorder, is there a higher percentage who have a co-existing diagnosis of endogenous depression than there is among clinic outpatients with posttraumatic stress disorder?"

Once the raw data for the above are ready for analysis by you or a computer, the next question is "Can the *null hypothesis* be rejected; that is, can the relationship you demonstrated (e.g., a positive correlation between cheating in college and cheating in medical school), or the proportions you obtained, be the product of chance?" Rephrased, the null hypothesis states "Your relationship (or comparison) is the result of chance."

Traditionally, a relationship or comparison is *statistically significant* if the probability of it occurring by chance is less than 5 out of 100 (1 out of 20). This is read as $P = <.05$. When P is $<.10$ but $>.05$, a statistical *trend* exists.

You should also know that for every 20 determinations that you make for statistical significance, regardless of the results one of these 20 determinations is likely to be statistically significant by chance. When this occurs (statistical significance is found, but no real life significance exists) it is a *type 1 error. Type 2 errors* occur when there is "real life" significance, but your statistical test, or the size of your sample, was insufficient to demonstrate a statistical significance.

Common tests of statistical significance include correlation analysis, regression analysis, t tests, ANOVA, and chi squared. *Correlation analysis* portrays, and determines the statistical significance of, the relationship between two variables. (A *variable* is something that can be measured and can vary, such as a National Bored Score, or a blood pressure.) One example of a question handled by correlation analysis is "What is the relationship between a medical school's National Bored Part 2 scores and the numbers of its graduates who enter residencies in psychiatry?" In one survey, the answer to that question was that the correlation (R) was 0.124, and the significance (P) was >.05, meaning that the probability of that relationship being due to chance was greater than 1 in 20. By tradition, we say the relationship was non-significant. There are two types of correlation coefficients, the *Pearson* and the *Spearman* coefficients. The Pearson coefficient is used when values of the variables are analyzed directly. The Spearman is used when the values are placed in a rank order, and the ranks (not the original values) are then analyzed.

A correlation can be portrayed as a *scattergram,* such as the one below:

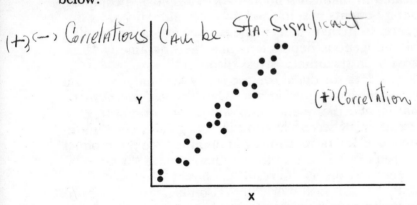

Strong Positive Correlation

In this example, as X increases, Y increases, This is a *positive correlation.* If, as X increases, Y decreases (or vice versa), there is a *negative correlation.* Negative correlations, as well as positive ones, can be significant. If, as X increases, there is no pattern of change in Y, *no correlation* exists. Correlation does not prove cause, only statistical association. The maximum positive correlation is $R = 1.0$ and the maximum negative correlation is $R = -1.0$. The "strength" of a correlation is the absolute value of R, not whether it is positive or negative.

Correlation is not synonymous with cause. For example, there is probably a high correlation between a city's ice cream sales and its drownings; however, it is a third variable, hot weather, that is probably causally related to each of the other two.

One means of using correlation to make inferences about cause is *regression analysis.* To understand regression analysis, you need to know that a *dependent variable* is one whose values are influenced, statistically or in real life, by other variables called *independent variables.* For example, factors influencing (the dependent variable of) how often a person malingers (fakes illness) probably include (the independent variables of) whether he has a condition called sociopathy and whether he enjoys his work. Regression analysis is used when multiple independent variables (e.g., sociopathic behaviors, alcoholic behaviors, drug dependency) are significantly correlated with a dependent variable (e.g., frequency of malingering) and you want to know which of these independent variables most strongly influences malingering.

t tests assess the significance of the difference between two means. For example, if the mean score on the National Boreds in Behavioral Sciences in 1989 for Chicago Medical School (CMS) students is 650, and for Harvard students 550, a t test would determine whether this difference is significant. *ANOVA (analysis of variance)* is used to assess the significance of the differences among three or more means. For example, if the mean score on the National Boreds in Behavioral Sciences in 1989 for CMS students is 650, for Yale students 600, for Harvard students 550, and for University of Illinois students 548, ANOVA would clarify whether the differences among these means are significant.

Chi squared assesses the significance of the difference between two or more proportions (percentages). For example, if 8% of 25 inpatients with posttraumatic stress disorder concurrently have endogenous depression, in contrast to only 4% of 25 clinic outpatients with posttraumatic stress disorder, chi squared analysis would assess whether the difference between the 8% and the 4% is significant.

To perform the above analyses, and to understand other statistical information, you should know certain definitions and concepts:

Frequency distributions are graphs with values of a variable on one axis, and the number of subjects manifesting each value of that variable on the other axis:

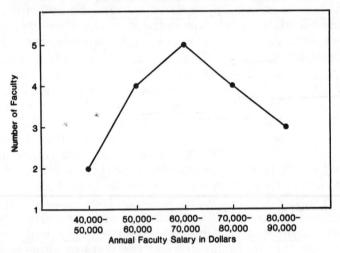

This can also be presented as a *histogram,* which is the same as the above, but using rectangles:

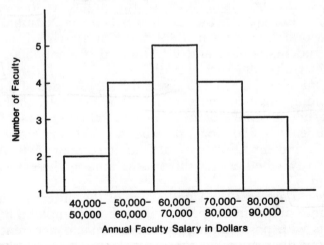

For each frequency distribution, there is a mean, mode and median. The *mean* is the average. The *mode* is the most common value. The *median* is the value "in the middle"; that is, half the values are higher, and half are lower.

Frequency distributions come in many shapes:

Normal distribution curves (*bell-shaped* or *Gaussian* curves) occur when the *sample size (N)* is huge and physiologic measurements (e.g., pulse, blood pressure) with multiple determinants (e.g., patient's age, weight, degree of anxiety) are made. The normal curve (below) is bell-shaped and symmetrical, and the mean, mode and median are identical:

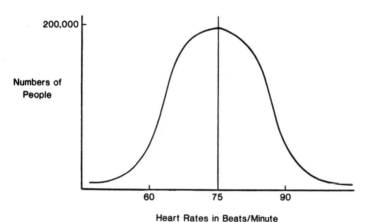

Heart Rates in Beats/Minute

A bell-shaped curve for the heart rates of people in a population

In statistical analyses, the *variability of values from the mean* (degree of "straying" or deviating from the mean) is important. One measure of variability is the *range,* which is the difference between the highest and lowest score. For example, on one psychiatry clerkship final examination, the range of scores was from 73% to 97% correct. Another measure of straying from the mean is *standard deviation of the mean,* which is better than range as a measure of straying from the mean because (by definition) it accounts for the deviation from the mean of *every* value recorded, and is thus less influenced by dramatically high or low values. The formula for standard deviation is

$$\sigma = \sqrt{\Sigma x^2 / N\text{-}1}$$

where σ is standard deviation, Σx^2 is the sum of the squares of the differences between each value and the mean, and N is the number of measurements.

For a normal distribution curve, 68% of values are between +1 and −1 standard deviations from the mean. 95% are between +2 and −2 standard deviations from the mean, and 99% are between +3 and −3 standard deviations from the mean. For example, let's say that the mean score for Indiana University students on the Physiology Boreds is 520, and the standard deviation is 10. This means that 68% of the students scored between 510 and 530, 95% between 500 and 540, and 99% from 490 to 550.

For another example, let's say that grades in the anatomy class at George Washington University are based upon how a student compares to the "curve." On her midterm, Mary Jones scores 80% correct. The class mean for the midterm is 70% and the standard deviation is 5. On her final, she scores 83% correct. The class mean on the final is 68% and the standard deviation is 10. Obviously, she scored better "against the curve" on her midterm (as she was two standard deviations above the mean) even though her raw score on the midterm was lower than her raw score on the final. To better assess how students perform on tests compared to the class mean, some departments give *Z scores,* based upon how many standard deviations a student scores above and below the mean.

A related measure of variability is *standard error of the mean.* This is the standard deviation of the mean divided by the square root of the number of people (N) sampled. The more people sampled, therefore, the less the standard error of the mean. In most research samples, frequency distributions are not normal curves. They are asymmetrical; i.e., they have a "skew." *Positive skew* occurs when the mean is on the left side of the curve, and the "long tail" occurs on the right side of the curve. *Negative skew* occurs when the mean is on the right and the "long tail" is on the left, as depicted below.

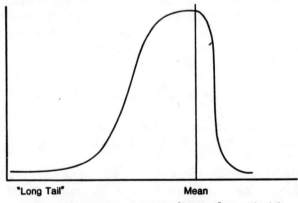

"Long Tail"   Mean

A curve with negative skew. The "long tail" is at the left.

Occasionally, a frequency distribution has two "humps," representing two separate tendencies within the sample. This is called a *bimodal distribution.* For example, professionals at a hospital were asked whether they liked their weekly supervisory rounds. It can be seen from the bimodal distribution below that their responses did not cluster about the mean, but instead indicated that many staff disliked the supervisory rounds, many liked them, and only a few were neutral.

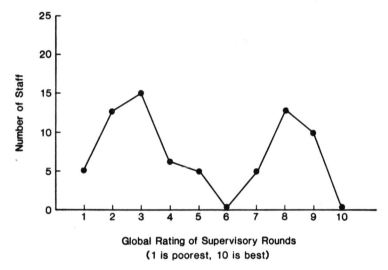

Global Rating of Supervisory Rounds
(1 is poorest, 10 is best)

Another concept pertinent to frequency distributions is *kurtosis,* which is how much that distribution is flat or "pointy."

Below are four distribution curves with different means but the same variability.

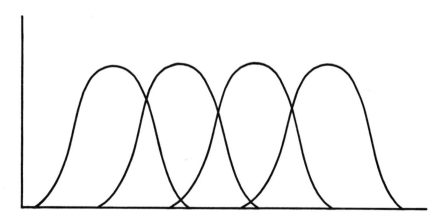

Next are four distribution curves with the same means but different variability (kurtosis):

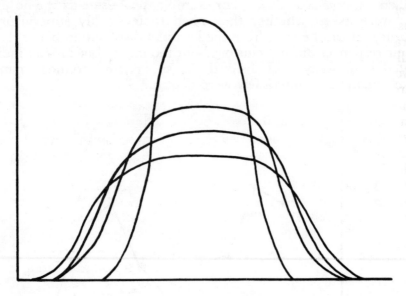

II. OTHER RESEARCH CONCEPTS

A. *Experiments*

Experiments are the best way to assess cause and effect. You *do* something to an *"experimental group"* of subjects, and compare the results to those for a *matched control group.* To minimize subject and investigator bias, *double blind experiments* are employed. In these, the subject and the investigator don't know whether the subject is getting the experimental or the control treatment.

B. *Prospective and Retrospective Studies*

1. *Prospective:* In a prospective study, your sample is chosen before it experiences the illness or treatment or other event to be studied. This is also called a *longitudinal* study, and the group studied is a *cohort.*

2. *Retrospective:* Your population is assessed *after* the event or illness or treatment to be studied. Retrospective studies are less expensive, less time-consuming, and more popular than prospective studies, but they are less useful in determining causality.

C. Sampling

In learning about a disorder it is ideal to study all people (the *population*) with that disorder. For example, to study what other psychiatric illnesses co-exist in Vietnam War veterans with post-traumatic stress disorder (PTSD), ideally you should interview all the 500,000 Vietnam War veterans with that disorder. This would include inpatients, outpatients and nonpatients (the latter are people who have PTSD who have not sought or received care for it). This is impossible, so *samples* (representative segments) of the population must be taken. At the Veterans Administration (V.A.) hospital in North Chicago, Illinois, we studied 25 *randomly* selected inpatients from the Stress Disorder Inpatient Treatment Unit, and 25 *consecutive* admissions to the outpatient group therapy program. This sampling is imperfect, because only patients were interviewed. But it minimized selection bias at our V.A. *Random sampling* may include using tables of random numbers, drawing numbers "from a hat" as long as the number drawn is replaced each time, or selecting every 10th or 100th (etc.) name from a complete alphabetical listing of a population to be surveyed.

In door-to-door surveys, one should randomly select houses in advance, taking care not to select only corner houses, or only midblock houses, as dwellers in these may be different from those on the block as a whole. If the respondent in a selected home is not initially available, and cannot be questioned on followup visits, the surveyor should not substitute another house, such as an adjacent house. By choosing adjacent houses, the skew would favor compliant respondents (who are different from noncompliant ones) much more than would standing pat with an entry of "nonresponder" in the ensuing statistical analysis and publication of results.

D. Epidemiologic Concepts

1. *Prevalence* is the number of cases of a disease or phenomenon in a population at a given time. For example, in door-to-door surveys in New Haven, Dr. Myrna Weissman's research group found a 0.4% population prevalence of schizophrenia.

2. *Incidence* is the number of new cases in a population per unit time, usually one year.

3. An *epidemic* occurs when the number of cases of an illness exceeds that expected for that population during the time period studied.

4. *Case fatality* rate is the percentage of patients with a given disease who die from it.

E. Reliability and Validity

1. *Reliability* measures the reproducibility or consistency of a test—the degree to which employing the same test twice on the same subject yields the same results.

For example, to establish reliability among investigators of a psychiatric diagnostic system, two doctors jointly interview the same patient, or separately examine the same patient within a day or two, and the degree to which they agree on mental status findings and diagnosis is called the *inter-rater reliability*. In psychiatry, the inter-rater reliability is usually measured by a statistic called *weighted kappa*. For another example, to determine reliability of a test instrument, sometimes the results from one half of the test are compared with those of the other half to see if the conclusions are similar; this is *split-half reliability*.

2. *Validity* is the degree that you are measuring what you want to measure. For example, the "Mini Mental State" examination, a screening test for dementia developed at the Johns Hopkins University, was shown to be valid because it highly correlated with computerized tomographic brain scan results of clinically demented people. This is an example of *concurrent validity*, the extent that results of testing using one instrument correlate with simultaneous functioning measured by other means. There are other kinds of validity. In *face validity*, it is "obvious" that you're measuring what you're supposed to measure. For example, giving anatomy students a test on muscles of the forearm which were taught that week appears to be a valid test of their knowledge of anatomy of the forearm muscles for that week. Another concept used by medical educators, *content validity*, is the degree to which a test instrument measures behaviors in the same proportions as they are valued. If, for example, a medical school course teaches two subjects in a certain proportion, then the examination should test the two subjects in the same proportion.

F. Diagnostic Confidence

Diagnostic confidence in a test is measured by its sensitivity and specificity. *Sensitivity* is the *true positive rate*, the proportion of patients with an illness (e.g., endogenous depression) who manifest abnormal results on a test (e.g., the dexamethasone suppression test) for that illness. In Dr. Bernard Carroll's 1981 study, the sensitivity of the dexamethasone suppression test for endogenous depression was 43%. The formula for sensitivity is:

$$\frac{\text{number of true positives x } 100}{\text{number of all cases with the illness}}$$

Supposing you wanted to study the sensitivity of a new laboratory test T for illness I. Of 125 patients with illness I, test T showed abnormal results in 75 cases. Of 50 patients who don't suffer from illness I, test T showed 10 abnormal results. Thus the sensitivity of test T for illness I is

$$\frac{75 \text{ x } 100}{125}$$

which is 60% in this example.

Specificity is the *true negative rate,* the proportion of people "without" an illness (e.g., people who don't have endogenous depression) who have normal results on a test (e.g., the dexamethasone suppression test) for that illness. In Carroll's study, the specificity of the dexamethasone suppression test for endogenous depression was 96%. The formula for specificity is:

$$\frac{\text{number of true negatives x } 100}{\text{number of all cases without the illness}}$$

Supposing you wanted to study the specificity of the same laboratory test T for the same illness I. You already have enough data, from the sensitivity example above, to compute the specificity of test T for illness I, which is

$$\frac{40 \text{ x } 100}{50}$$

which is 80% in this example.

Chapter 2:

MEDICAL SOCIOLOGY

Medical sociology is the social science which studies how belonging to various classes or groups influences the definition, frequency, symptomatology, diagnosis, treatment and prognosis of illness. A review such as this best centers about key concepts. A *social class* is a group of people with similar economic opportunities and prestige. The prestige associated with social class is called *socioeconomic status,* a term which is often used synonymously with social class. One means of "measuring" social class is Dr. August Hollingshead's *three factor index of social position,* consisting of occupation, education and residence. When Hollingshead's *two factor index* is used, the factors are occupation and education. In a *caste system,* social classes are formalized and fixed. India used to have such a system. India's previous castes are now social classes, with some interclass mobility.

Social mobility is a person's capacity to move upward or downward in the social class system. The best way to move *upward* is to obtain lots of education and defer gratification; e.g., a child of a carpenter goes to medical school. One way to move *downward* is to develop a chronic disabling illness; one example is that schizophrenic men are of lower socioeconomic class than their fathers. Of course, social-class related factors such as poor prenatal and obstetrical care (associated with lower socioeconomic status) can predispose to schizophrenia. Social mobility and social changes in this country are considerable and cause conflict between generations.

14

An *ethnic group* is a group of people with common national origin, religion, customs, language and (often) physical characteristics. *Ethnocentrism* is the belief that one's ethnic group has unique, special characteristics. *Prejudice* is "pre-judging" people without proper information. It diminishes self-esteem of the victim, increases his own prejudice, can serve as a *self-fulfilling prophecy* ("They say I am incompetent, so I must be incompetent"), and is often associated with *stereotypes.* A stereotype is a "blanket" misperception about groups of people, occasionally based upon valid studies of statistical differences, with the consequent inaccurate assumptions that most or all members of a group have certain characteristics. Prejudice can be increased by previous discrimination, by identifiability of groups, and by the capacity of those groups to retaliate against each other. Prejudice can be diminished by people working towards common goals at equal status, by enactment of laws, by integration, by education, and by availability of members of different groups to each other.

Adorno portrayed an *authoritarian personality* which he associated with prejudiced people: they tend to have conventional attitudes, require external supports, be very sensitive to issues of dominance, agree uncritically with dominant group authorities, react punitively to those who violate conventional norms, manifest intellectual rigidity, be cynical, use the defense mechanism of projection, show repression of sexuality, have an unusual interest in the sexual behavior of others, and be politically conservative.

A *role* is a situation (e.g., doctor, father, patient) which confers certain rights and places certain obligations upon a person. *Role conflict* occurs when a person occupies two simultaneous roles (e.g., when a relative asks a doctor for a prescription) whose demands are conflicting (e.g., one wants to help a relative but a doctor usually should not prescribe for his/her relatives). In Dr. Talcott Parsons' concept of the *sick role,* (an accepted, temporary deviation from the usual course of life), the patient is excused from potentially exacerbating (illness-worsening) obligations, and is expected to want help and to seek technically competent help. The extent to which a sick individual enters the sick role is affected by the obviousness of his signs and symptoms, the degree to which his illness disrupts the activity of his family, his life, and his motivation to participate in his usual activities, and his ability to tolerate his symptoms and signs.

Dr. Alexander Leighton studied *sociocultural disintegration,* a situation where members of a community become more susceptible to illness. Characteristics of sociocultural disintegration include poverty, frequent migration, impaired communications systems, increases in population, lack of leadership, "broken" homes, *anomie* (absence of cultural standards, called *norms*), increases in hostility, crime and violence, rising crime rates, increasing stress, and a vicious cycle with worse health maintenance services and more illness, including child abuse, addiction, tuberculosis, venereal disease, viral hepatitis (infection of the liver) and many other medical conditions.

A *reference group* is a group (e.g., college professors, work buddies, suburban matriarchs, members of a gang, Russians) to whom one looks for standards of behavior.

The *family* is the basic unit of reproduction, support, nurturing, transmission of cultural norms, and utilization of goods and services. It is the commonest source of referrals to doctors. Despite its nurturance, ideally it does not seek permanent intergenerational dependency of its members on each other. A *nuclear family* consists of a mother and father (in a 2-parent household) and their children. An *extended family* is a three-generation family. A *household* is all people in one dwelling unit. A *primary family* is one where the head of the family is the head of the household. A *secondary family* is one where the head of the family is not the head of the household (e.g., where a married couple with their child live in the home of their in-laws). Professionals who practice family psychotherapy as part of the treatment of patients with psychiatric illness believe that in many cases family relationships play a major part in causing and maintaining that illness. Consequently, family therapists treat the family as the patient, not just the person referred as the patient (the *identified patient*). This *defocusing* of the attention and criticism from the identified patient to the whole family is thought to be supportive and therapeutic for the identified patient.

People tend to marry people of similar socioeconomic status, religion, location of residence, attitudes, and personality traits. When similar personality traits influence marital choice, this is called *assortative mating.* When a married couple experiences a major attitudinal difference, they have two possible courses: to avoid facing the problem, or to develop a strategy for diminishing the strain. The risk of mental illness is decreased for married people, and death rates are lower for married persons.

Divorce is more common among people whose parents divorced, who married in their teens, and who are poor. It occurs regardless of whether there are children. In the U.S., there is significant marital instability, with *marriage rates* of 10/1000 per year and *divorce rates* of 4.8/1000 per year. In part because of divorce rates, the average mortgage duration is 4 years.

The *definition of illness* varies from society to society. *Deviant behavior* is not necessarily symptomatic of disease. When deviance is attributed to disease, the patient's problems are referred to doctors, thereby diminishing conflict with the social system. In Russia, this has reached a point of absurdity, with some dissidents (e.g., Medvedev) involuntarily hospitalized and medicated for their beliefs. Just as deviance can have multiple causes, *conformity* can be a sign of normality, excessive passivity, neurosis, and mental illness in general.

Compliance (cooperation) with medical recommendations has multiple determinants, including perceived severity of illness, complexity of the medical regimen, age, gender, social class, satisfaction with the physician, and physician's time spent with the patient. For chronic illness, simplicity of the treatment regimen is particularly important. Also fostering compliance are believing ① that one is sick, ② that the treatment will help, and ③ that the treatment has been properly explained. Physicians are often ignorant about their patients' compliance, and their overconfidence is sometimes rationalized on the basis of their clinical experience, regardless of their age.

There is an extensive literature on the *health-related characteristics of people of low socioeconomic status*, which can best be summarized by the quote attributed to Sophie Tucker: "I've been rich, and I've been poor. Rich is better." This is elaborated in Table 1.

TABLE 1: HEALTH-RELATED CHARACTERISTICS OF PEOPLE OF LOW SOCIOECONOMIC STATUS

I. *Family and social factors*

— Higher rates of parental death, separation and divorce
— Higher rates of job-related death
— More maternal household heads
— Increased competition for the attention of the single parent

More marriage at earlier ages
Greater sex role differentiation, with more distinctions in
who performs which family tasks, and who has higher
status
Less joint participation of both parents in leisure activities
Less chance of children learning to delay gratifications
Membership in fewer organizations
Greater reliance on nonverbal cues

II. *Primary Prevention*

Less knowledge and sophistication about human physiology
and pathology
Lower chance of eating a balanced diet
Less chance of obtaining health checkups costing money, or
to get free polio vaccine
Less chance of going for preventive health visits
Less orthodontic care

III. *Prevalence of Illness*

Higher infant mortality due to numerous causes
More premature birth
More of the following:
Mental retardation
Obesity
Chronic illness
High blood pressure
Blindness
Speech problems
Lung disease
Tuberculosis
Venereal (sexually-transmitted) disease
Mental illness in general, and specifically
psychosis
sociopathy
schizophrenia
Briquet's syndrome
More homicide, rape and robbery
More psychological dependency
Lower self esteem
Greater fears of change

IV. *Sick Role Behavior*

Greater responsiveness to crises than to future objectives
Diminished adherence to time-bound schedules
Less interest in medical care when ill
Less chance of self-referral to doctors when ill
More self-medication
Greater chance of using nonmedical personnel for treatment
Less trust of the health care system
Being relatively sicker once admitted to the hospital
Greater likelihood of systemic/somatic presentation of mental illness
Greater chance of being treated on a hospital ward by a "committee" of housestaff and students
Longer hospital stays
Lower life expectancy

In contrast, Dr. Robert Coles and many other authors have eloquently described that, despite the above, the poor have a considerable capacity for acting with dignity and wisdom in the face of adversity. Also, in the United States currently, the poor now make as many doctor visits (corrected for illness) as do their better-off counterparts. The poor have a greater tolerance for family members with behavioral or characterologic deviance. The poor are less likely than the middle class to abuse marijuana. Studies from the 1950s concluded that "neurotic" disorders were less common among people of lower socioeconomic status, but this finding has not been replicated since then. Mania and endogenous depression are distributed equally among the social classes.

Concerning *ethnic groups and illness,* according to some (not all) studies white Anglo-Saxon Protestants, Irish-Americans, and Chicano blue collar workers are more stoic in response to illness than are Italian-Americans and Jewish-Americans. The frequency of coronary artery disease is lower for Japanese in Japan than it is for Japanese-Americans in Hawaii, for whom the frequency is lower than for Japanese-Americans in California. There are several possible explanations, including personality characteristics, diet, and cultural stresses. American blacks are more prone to hypertension, prostate cancer, coma (unconsciousness) in childhood resulting from accidents such as falling from unscreened apartment windows, homicide victimization, sickle cell anemia, certain thalassemias, and sarcoidosis. Sickle cell anemia and thalassemia are conditions with excessive breakdown of red blood cells. Sarcoidosis is a multiple-system condition which, under the microscope, looks similar to tuberculosis. For endogenous depression, the symptoms and signs are the same worldwide, except for delusional content and degree of guilt.

Concerning *occupational illnesses,* doctors are less likely than their age-matched counterparts to get checkups, or to visit doctors when seriously ill. Female physicians are more prone to commit suicide than their age-matched counterparts. Doctors in non-direct-patient care specialties are more prone to behavioral problems than those who care directly for patients. The high status of doctors is related to their control over their workplace, their professional licensure, extensive education and high incomes. Dr. David Hilfiker movingly describes the emotionally-charged nature of the doctor-patient relationship, as doctors deal with intensely personal issues, physically examine their patients, are relied upon heavily, are expected to be excellent at diagnosis and treatment, and are expected to be caring and readily-available.

Radiologists are more prone to developing cancer, farmers to getting low back injuries, plastics workers to acquiring hepatic disease, policemen to suicide, prizefighters to complications of head injury, professional athletes to bone and joint injuries, professional writers to bipolar disorder, asbestos workers to mesothelioma (a type of cancer), automobile mechanics to lead poisoning, and coal miners to anthracosis (black lung). In general, mining has a very high rate of accidental death. Obtaining work, family and social histories from patients can facilitate rapport, compliance, and diagnosis and inform the physician and social worker what social supports are available. Job satisfaction is positively correlated with life expectancy.

Folk medicine is the practice of healing outside the medical establishment or in the absence of a medical establishment. Folk medicine's contributions to traditional medicine include trephining (removal of a disc of bone), bone-setting, removal of ovaries, obstetrics including Caesarian section, laparotomy (surgical exploration of the abdomen), uvulectomy, comparative anatomy, autopsy, cautery, inoculation, baths, inhalations, laxatives, enemas, ointments, the antimalarial drug quinine, the nerve conduction blocker curare, the bronchodilating drug ephedrine, the blood pressure-lowering chemical rauwolfia, and the cardiac-assisting medication digitalis. Also from folk medicine are ethyl alcohol, the narcotic analgesic opium, the topical eye anesthetic cocaine, and (of no inherent value) the hallucinogen mescaline.

Folk (and medical) theories of illness can be divided into *personalistic* and *naturalistic*. In the former, illness is thought to be the product of a person's relationship to his environment. In the latter, illness is thought to result from an imbalance of nature (e.g., body humors, "yin" and "yang") in the body. Beliefs about illness causality are strongly held and not readily discarded even when two cultures come in close contact. All modern societies have an incest taboo, ceremonies for birth, marriage and death, an option to breastfeed, and rules for toilet behavior.

Folk healers are sometimes helpful. Alegria's description of Chicano *"curanderas* (curers)"* includes that they tend to be retired women over 40 whose offices are in their homes. They charge fees of $3 to $8, treat mild common complaints, culture-based illnesses, and medical conditions treated by doctors with unacceptable results. In starting a medical care center in a community, it is important for the planners to know about the local folk beliefs, folk healers, and health needs, and include local representatives in the planning process.

There are small but significant positive correlations between the sum of one's *life change events* and the development of illnesses of all sorts. These events (e.g., death of a spouse, son or daughter leaving home) are easy to define, are given points (the most points are for death of a spouse), and are summed for prediction purposes. Not all these events are sad or negative; for example, the birth of a child also constitutes a stress. Different categories of people (e.g., men vs. women, young vs. old) are affected differently by life events. The stress-illness correlation sometimes confuses cause and effect, and rejects individual susceptibilities which include genetics, intrauterine influences, effects of diet and the physical environment, and past experience. Previous illness is a better predictor of future illness than is the sum of life change points.

The better a doctor-patient relationship, the better the patient compliance, the better the prognosis of a given illness, and the lower the chance of doctor-shopping and lawsuits. Regarding "frightening" of patients by doctors or health authorities, fear-containing messages (e.g., "High-salt diets predispose to hypertension.") are best conveyed concurrently with helpful recommendations (e.g., "Here is how to prepare a low-salt diet."). Many physicians prefer patients with well-documented illnesses, positive laboratory findings, good compliance with (and response to) treatment, and supportive families. When patients do not fall into these categories, when they have complicated social problems, or when they manifest hypochondriasis or Briquet's syndrome, these same physicians are more apt to label the patient as a "crock" or "dingbat" in hospital-corridor conversations.

A number of social psychology studies are relevant to medical practice: Rosenthal's concept of the *"self-fulfilling prophecy"* is that people sometimes act upon others' spoken and unspoken expectations of them, so that if one expects a student to do badly, this often is conveyed to the student, who is then more prone to doing badly. The *Hawthorne effect* is when a work environment change (e.g., increase or dimming of lighting) is made that workers believe is for their benefit, they will work more productively regardless of the content of the change.

The *Stanton-Schwartz phenomenon* is that when staff is in covert disagreement about the care of a patient, that patient is more prone to developing uncontrollable, excited behavior. Patient care improves when professionals of different disciplines work well together and communicate clearly, when admissions to treatment units are relatively open, and when secondary and tertiary prevention efforts take priority over custodial functions.

Chapter 3:

HEALTH CARE DELIVERY

I. OVERALL DESCRIPTION FROM A MEDICAL POINT OF VIEW

The phrase health care delivery is a modern one that implies that maintenance of health is more than just doctors and nurses treating sick people. It implies a complex system with strong socioeconomic influences.

Nevertheless, what doctors and nurses do treat deserves discussion. The *most common acute medical problems* are, in descending order of frequency, upper respiratory conditions, influenza, and injuries. The ten *most common surgical procedures* are, in descending order, diagnostic dilatation and curettage ("D and C") of the uterus, hysterectomy, tonsillectomy, sterilization of women, hernia repair, oophorectomy (removal of one or both ovaries), Caesarian section, gallbladder removal, muscle surgery and setting of fractures. Five of the seven most common are performed only on women. The frequencies with which surgical procedures are performed for a given reason vary considerably among nations. For example, the 1981 American Caesarian section rate was 50–200% higher than that of all other countries except Canada & Australia.

The *leading reasons for office visits* are, in descending order, general examination, routine prenatal examination, throat problems, diagnosis and management of hypertension, postoperative visits, cough, head cold, upper respiratory infection, back symptoms, skin rash and gynecologic examination. In 1978, there were about 4.8 physician visits per person, and about 75% of the population made at least one visit. Seventy-eight percent of the total visits took place in a physician's office, 15% in a hospital clinic or emergency room, and less than 1% as a "house call (home visit)."

Almost 70% of *hospital discharge diagnoses* (the diagnosis given in a patient's chart when he is discharged from the hospital) are accounted for (in descending order) by the following 6 diagnostic groups: diseases of the circulatory system and digestive system; complications of pregnancy; accidents, poisoning and violence; and problems of the genitourinary and respiratory systems. Diagnosis-specific lengths of hospital stay have been declining for many illnesses for many reasons, including better therapeutics and the "D.R.G.s," which we will discuss later.

The *conditions that most commonly limit people's activity* are, in descending order, diseases of the musculoskeletal system, circulatory system, nervous system and organs of special sense, respiratory system and mental disorders. 14.2% of the population had limitation of activity due to chronic conditions. Physicians should be aware that dental cavities are among the most common health care problems, even in light of "preventive dentistry."

The *10 leading causes of death* in 1979 were, in descending order, heart disease, cancer, stroke (cerebral vascular accident), accidents, chronic obstructive pulmonary disease, influenza, pneumonia (infection of the lung), diabetes mellitus, cirrhosis (degeneration and deformity) of the liver, suicide, and perinatal (before, during and after childbirth) conditions. As for most categories of disease, behaviors play an important role in the prevention, causation and recovery from these disorders. Exercise, diet, use of seat belts and adherence to speed limits, avoidance of smoking and substance abuse, proper treatment of depression, and compliance with proper drug regimens are all highly effective preventative efforts.

To care for all the above conditions, the average physician works about 50 hours per week, 90% of which is in direct patient care. The average physician has about 130 visits per week, about 90 in the office and about 40 in the hospital. The range is from 55 visits per week for psychiatrists to 180 for general practitioners.

II. ACHIEVEMENTS OF THE AMERICAN HEALTH CARE SYSTEM

By many parameters, health care in the U.S. has been significantly improving, and is of high quality. Our technological excellence is particularly noteworthy.

The *crude mortality rate* for the population was 8.8/1000 per year in the early 1980s, compared to the steady 9.4–9.5 from 1950 to 1970. Please note that for given areas or states (e.g., Florida), crude mortality rate is not as useful an indicator of health as is *age-adjusted mortality* (e.g., there is a high number of elderly in Florida). *Infant mortality* has been decreasing, with influences including family planning, better prenatal and perinatal care, and higher birth weights. *Maternal mortality* has been decreasing, some contributing factors including increased use of prenatal services and legalized abortion. There is a decreasing *child mortality* between the ages of 1 and 4, which has been the most dramatic of all the influences upon national mortality rates and life expectancies.

Age-adjusted death rates have decreased, and *life expectancies* have significantly increased. Decreasing death rates have been noted for heart disease, cerebrovascular disease, accidents, influenza and pneumonia, diabetes and arteriosclerosis (lipid-containing occlusion of the arteries). Mortality rates have improved particulary for blacks and Native Americans (American Indians). The poor now have a greater access to health care than they did in the 1940s, 50s and 60s. Reasons for the above improvements have included better technology and better public health measures, which include primary, secondary and tertiary prevention. *Primary prevention* is the prevention of the occurrence of an illness. *Secondary prevention* is early detection of illness. *Tertiary prevention* is reduction of disability once the illness is "established." In *active prevention* strategies, the individual must do something (e.g., follow a certain diet) to promote his health. In *passive prevention* (e.g., pasteurization and dating of milk) the individual simply *receives* the benefit.

In the past 200 years, most major improvements in our population's health resulted from better nutrition, water purification, sanitary sewage disposal, and communicable disease control. Dramatic changes in incidence and prevalence of certain diseases (e.g., the decline in prevalence of tuberculosis in Massachusetts from 1850 to 1890) can occur independently from medical or surgical treatment (e.g., prescription of streptomycin for tuberculosis). Ninety percent of cancers have thus far been shown to be related to environmental factors. An estimated 40% of cancers could be controlled by changing the environment, such as by anti-smoking campaigns, cutting down by physicians on the use of chest x-rays as a routine screening measure, removal of asbestos from heating ducts in buildings, and limitations on the production and emission of carcinogenic toxins such as nuclear wastes and dioxin. Further, some studies show that the efficacy of such predominantly-social interventions as home health care for certain conditions can be as good as or better than "state-of-the-art" treatment programs such as intensive care units.

Curiously, because of these well-publicized improvements in indices of American health and well-publicized state-of-the-art technology, because of high values placed on physical fitness, and because of raised expectations created by the *"medicalization"* of suffering (e.g., fat suction surgery for obesity, crisis counseling for trauma victims), a paradox exists: Although on the whole Americans' health has improved, more Americans are dissatisfied with their health than in previous decades.

Despite the above, our health care is not the best in the world for any of the major health parameters. For example, people in Sweden, France and the Netherlands have a higher life expectancy at birth. Sweden, the Netherlands and Canada have lower infant mortality rates. Russia has a better *physician-to-patient ratio.* Our maternal mortality rates are not the best in the world either.

Large numbers of American children are still unimmunized. Twelve percent of deaths are *sentinel deaths*, meaning deaths which could have been prevented by timely, proper medical intervention. Not all people benefit equally from health care. There are approximately 16 million people in *doctor-shortage areas,* 9 million of whom are in rural areas and 7 million in inner cities. Construction of acute hospitals and influxes of doctors tend to occur in expanding high-income areas, and more specialists practice in metropolitan areas. Washington, D.C. has about 360 physicians per 100,000 population, whereas South Dakota has 81 per 100,000 population. In the South, particularly Appalachia, there is a lower life expectancy at birth.

Our system overemphasizes disease and underemphasizes health and primary prevention. Yet, according to Banta and White (in Dr. Steven Jonas' informative textbook *Health Care*

Delivery in the United States) perhaps 80% of our treatments do not have controlled clinical trials to document that they are helpful. For example, for decades the various psychotherapies have been thought to be helpful in the treatment of most psychiatric (and some "nonpsychiatric") illnesses, but only for a small proportion of these therapies (e.g., cognitive psychotherapy for certain types of "major depression") have well-controlled trials been done to demonstrate their efficacy as a primary treatment of a well-defined psychiatric disorder.

Also, in many ways to be enumerated later in this chapter, in the past two decades the health care field has become *destabilized;* i.e., it has lost much of the socioeconomic stability that characterized it in the previous two decades. The environment and ethics of medical care are changing and will continue to change.

III. INFLUENCES OF SOCIOECONOMIC FACTORS

Although advances in medicine are incorporated into the culture and demanded by patients, and although the physician's practice has in the past not been fully subject to conventional market forces, in many ways the health care system mirrors society. The *Civil Rights Movement* of the '60s and '70s had a significant influence. *Medicaid* provided funds for the medically-indigent. *Affirmative Action* led to the hiring of more minority group members and women in medical occupations. The *community mental health movement* (although partially a failure because of most communities' disinterest in effectively incorporating and integrating many of the discharged mental patients, and because many of the patients' recoveries were only temporary for a number of reasons) helped change the care of many psychiatric inpatients from a custodial role. This led to large numbers of discharges to the community *(deinstitutionalization)*. The latter was initially facilitated by the utilization of neuroleptic drugs such as chlorpromazine. *Medicare* allowed many poor people to receive hemodialysis (extracorporeal pump-driven membrane filtration of the blood leading to removal of "uremic" toxic substances and normalization of electrolyte levels).

For the aging, the mandatory retirement age for certain jobs was raised to 70. An *Age Discrimination Act* was passed which established penalties for discrimination on the basis of age. The Association of American Medical Colleges established an employment pool for emeritus health science professors.

The federal government has strongly supported the admission of women to medical school, and women now constitute 33% of medical school first year classes. Perhaps for the first time, some medical school teaching is done on gender-related psychology. More time and attention have been given to the subjects of rape, spouse abuse, and therapeutic abortion.

For children, a *Child Abuse Reporting Act* was passed, and children can now be treated for venereal (sexually-transmitted) disease without parental consent. The handicapped have benefited from requirements for special facilities for the handicapped. The mentally ill were affected by *right-to-treatment* court decisions whereby professionals responsible for involuntarily hospitalized patients were required to provide more than custodial care. Students were given access to documents (such as letters of recommendation, grades and memoranda) about them because of the *Buckley Amendment*. Research subjects were protected to some extent by *institutional review boards.* However, despite Jefferson's 18th Century references to the importance of health for the population, there are no references to health in the United States Constitution.

There have been significant changes in the *doctor-patient relationship,* particularly when physicians are inattentive to the patients' individual needs. When there is good doctor-patient rapport, there is more patient compliance and satisfaction. The frequency of lawsuits has been dramatically increasing, to the point where some specialists (e.g., neurosurgeons in Long Island) are paying $80,000–$100,000 annually in malpractice insurance. Many doctors consequently practice *defensive medicine* with its excessive use of tests, elaborate informed consent procedures, detailed, meticulous charting, and other cautions. Many patients "doctor-shop" if their needs are not met. There is a significant national push for more primary care physicians.

Economically, continued *inflation* has been a major problem, with some dramatic steps recently taken because of government, insurance company, and public perceptions that the medical profession has not sufficiently curbed its costs. In fiscal 1980, the United States spent over $240 billion, 9% of its Gross National Product, on health care services.

The massive inflation was particularly influenced by rises in hospital care costs, especially personnel costs, the most expensive item in a hospital's budget. (The more expensive technology a hospital uses, the lower the percentage of hospital costs that are spent for personnel. For high-technology cancer centers, the figure may be about 40% for personnel, and for some large psychiatric hospitals the figure could be 80%). There are multiple factors contributing to inflation: Perhaps 67% of medical costs are paid by *"third party payers"* (e.g., government agencies like Medicare, or insurance companies), so neither the doctor nor the patient must be cost-conscious in many circumstances. Further, the United States has the highest national rate of malpractice insurance, which translates into higher fees. Not all hospitals are equally cost-conscious; in one survey, there was a 17-fold variance in the cost of the same laboratory tests. Advanced, specialized laboratory tests are usually very expensive. Larger numbers of physicians enter specialties and subspecialties, and specialists charge higher fees. For example, dermatologists charge more for the treatment of a given rash than do family practitioners. The population is aging, and the aged require more care for their multisystem disease and multiple medications.

There are more physicians, and physicians and other health manpower create their own demand (an example of supply generating demand). New and existing hospital beds create demands for care and administrative pressure for occupancy: "A built bed is a filled bed," because empty beds are a major cause of money loss. Thus, *bed utilization* does not exactly reflect need for hospitalization, although this relationship is changing with the use of DRGs, which will be discussed shortly. Physician fees are rarely subject to competitive market forces. Finally, as the population becomes more urbanized, fees rise, as the higher the physician-to-population ratio, the higher the fees.

Dramatic strategies for reducing inflation in health care costs have included the following: Many insurance companies and government agencies (such as the Veterans Administration) have been reimbursing hospitals for patient care based upon diagnosis *(diagnosis related groups, called DRGs)*, not length of stay. A hypothetical example would be a third party payer giving $2500 to a hospital for the inpatient care of a patient undergoing the removal of an inflamed appendix, regardless of the length of his hospital stay.

Also, some third party payers are establishing *preferred provider organizations (P.P.O.s)*, whereby groups of physicians bid for access to reimbursement. All things being equal, the low bidder is eligible for the reimbursement. Many third party payers, including the government, are raising their *deductible* costs and increasing their requirements for *co-payments*. Recently, Blue Shield (a very heavily utilized non-profit health insurance plan) of Massachusetts began a pilot program in which obstetricians receive larger fees if their patients have below-average lengths of stay in the hospital, as long as these lengths of stay are within acceptable standards. Another cost-controlling attempt, now being phased out, is *regionalization* of the control of health care, with quasi-governmental agencies limiting whether hospitals can be built and what expensive technologies (e.g., computerized tomographic scans) they may use.

IV. THE PAYMENT OF HEALTH CARE COSTS

About 89% of the population has some government, private, or Blue Cross/Blue Shield health care insurance coverage. About 11% (about 21.5 million people as of 1986) do not, most commonly the recently employed or fired, farm workers, or people on maternity leave. Although *third party payment* is inflationary, it has given more people access to care, especially hospital care. *Medicare* stands for "medical care for the aged," but also covers people on railroad retirement, social security disability and chronic dialysis. The latter is an excellent example of *"catastrophic coverage."* Medicare was proposed in Kennedy's "New Frontier," and passed into law in Johnson's "Great Society" Administration as a 1965 amendment to the Social Security Law. The cost is borne by the Federal Government, which now asks for some co-payments by patients, and which has begun using a D.R.G. system. Its day-to-day business is handled by Blue Cross/Blue Shield. The state's roles in Medicare are minimal and limited to hospital inspection functions. The founders of Medicare explicitly stated that Medicare was not going to tell doctors how and where to care for patients. However, Medicare has influenced styles of patient care. For example, it will not pay for care in a private or state psychiatric hospital, so that doctors and their elderly psychiatric patients relying on Medicare must utilize the psychiatric ward of a general hospital. Of course, the latter is an excellent site for inpatient hospital care.

Like Medicare, *Medicaid* was proposed during the Kennedy Administration and passed into law during the Johnson Administration as a 1965 amendment to the Social Security Law. It had a precursor in the 1930s. Medicaid is medical care for the poor. Full payment is given to the blind and disabled, elderly poor people, and families with dependent children when a parent is unemployed, cannot work, or absent. Costs are borne jointly by state governments and the Federal Government according to a variety of formulas. Curiously, prior to 1981, Arizona chose not to participate in Medicaid. The combined cost of Medicare and Medicaid is over 84 billion annually, each far in excess of federal funds spent for research, which in turn far exceeds federal funds given for training.

The *Uniformed Services Health Benefits Program (U.S.B.H.P.)* is our system of payment for military personnel and their dependents. One component of the U.S.B.H.P. program is the *Civilian Health and Medical Program of the Uniformed Services (C.H.A.M.P.U.S.)*, which covers the spouses and other dependents of military personnel when this care is not available at the local military health care facility.

In *prepaid health* care plans and health maintenance organizations *(H.M.O.s)*, treatment is offered to a defined population. The subscriber pays a fixed amount to a multispecialty group providing most basic and primary care medical services. (Please note that not all prepaid health care plans are H.M.O.s.) Examples include Kaiser-Permanente and H.I.P. (Health Insurance Plan of New York City). As of 1979 there were about 210 prepaid health plans, serving approximately 8 million Americans, and the figure keeps increasing dramatically. Advantages to physicians participating in H.M.O.s include a regular work schedule, a reasonably good salary, benefits such as malpractice insurance, good access to ancillary services, and a "collegial" atmosphere. Disadvantages include some loss of autonomy and income resulting from working as a salaried employee, and (in H.M.O.s which give bonuses to physicians who make fewer referrals to specialists, and who order fewer expensive laboratory tests) a conflict of interest between thoroughness of patient care and extent of the physician's personal income. Advantages to patients include some emphasis on preventive care, and a trend towards reducing the number of hospitalizations. Further, there are no charges at times of service, and there is "one stop shopping" often available 24 hours daily, continuity of care, and some protection against unnecessary surgery. However, patients joining H.M.O.s may have to switch doctors, losing continuity of care with a familiar physician, if their pre-H.M.O. doctor is not affiliated with the H.M.O.

Historically, third-party payers have discriminated against psychiatric patients. For example, only 50% of outpatient psychiatric care is reimbursed by private insurers and Blue Cross/ Blue Shield, compared to 80% for "med/surg" patients. However, in 1989 California passed into law the requirement that patients with schizophrenia, bipolar disorder, endogenous depression with psychosis, and infantile autism be reimbursed by the same standards as are "med/surg" patients. Hopefully, this will set a national precedent.

We will not discuss private health care coverage other than to say that it allows for the costs of hospitalization to be divided among multiple subscribers.

V. INFLUENTIAL ORGANIZATIONS IN THE HEALTH CARE SYSTEM

There are many very influential organizations in our complex health care system. These include the U.S. Department of Health and Human Services, the Veterans Administration, city and state departments of health and departments of registration and education, the American Medical Association (A.M.A.), the National Medical Association, the Association of American Medical Colleges (A.A.M.C.), the National Board of Medical Examiners, the Educational Council for Foreign Medical Graduates (E.C.F.M.G.), the Coordinating Committee on Medical Education (C.C.M.E.), and the J.C.A.H.

For a variety of reasons, we will only discuss the *J.C.A.H.* (the *Joint Commission on Accreditation of Hospitals*). This agency accredits hospitals to receive Medicare, Medicaid and Blue Cross/ Blue Shield payments. J.C.A.H. inspects each hospital at least every two years, and grants full or probationary accreditation. It assesses charting, infection control, the physical plant, supervision, protection of research subjects, informed consent, granting of privileges, and physical safety. The "bottom line" for this is *quality assurance,* which is defined thus: "There should be evidence of a well-defined, organized program designed to enhance patient care through the ongoing objective assessment of important aspects of patient care and the correction of identified problems." The J.C.A.H. can support the granting of hospital privileges to dentists, dietitians, oral surgeons, osteopaths, psychologists, and other types of health professionals.

With continuing inflation of health care costs, with many individuals subject to financial ruin in the event of prolonged severe illness, and with inequities in the quality of health care available to people of different means, additional or alternative national health programs have been proposed. These include A) compulsory insurance for *catastrophic illnesses* funded by employers and by taxation; B) compulsory insurance for most medical services including nursing home care, funded as in item A with fees negotiated between local medical societies and local governments (as is done in Canada); C) a national health service in which physicians are salaried government employees, physician distribution by location & specialty is determined by the government, and allocation of finite medical resources is made by the government.

VI. PROVIDERS OF HEALTH CARE: HOSPITALS, AMBULATORY SERVICES, PHYSICIANS AND OTHER PROVIDERS

Historically, *hospitals* developed in poorhouses as places to die, and the majority who entered died. In our "modern" time, less than 5% of those who enter hospitals die. As most uncomplicated infections have been "conquered," hospitals now primarily cope with the pathology of degenerative diseases, neoplasms (benign tumors and cancer) and trauma. There are now over 7000 hospitals with over 1.5 million beds and a *mean hospital occupancy rate* about 75% and sinking, with some hospitals closing during the past several years because of bankruptcy. The average hospital has 225 beds, but most are under 200 beds. An important recent trend has been the widespread construction and purchasing of hospitals by for-profit corporations such as Hospital Corporation of America and Humana. These corporations have made large profits because of cost-effective measures such as mass purchasing. They have also been at the forefront of the medical profession's recent utilization of mass advertising and marketing techniques.

There are considerable local variations in the types of medical or surgical procedures done, influenced by the numbers of surgeons, the numbers of hospital beds, and the type of third party coverage available.

Committees help to run hospitals. Hospitals are expected to have infection control committees, pharmacy and therapeutics committees, surgery and pathology tissue committees, medical records committees and utilization review (Are the hospital's beds being used appropriately?) committees. According to Rogatz and to Jonas, the future of hospitals includes more external regulation, more ambulatory surgery, more home care services, more long-term care facilities, special housing for the elderly, more H.M.O.s and hospices, and less "tyranny of the bed (emphasis on bed occupancy)."

Nursing homes are increasing in number. There are over 18,000 homes with over 1,350,000 beds, the average number of beds being 90. About 70% of the occupants are women, and 85% of the occupants are over 65 with a mean age of 78 and a mean length of stay of 2.7 years. Occupancy rates and employee-patient ratios are increasing, as are the numbers and proportions of psychiatric patients.

In *hospices,* which care for dying patients, the patient's sense of well-being has priority over the prolongation of his life. Among other facets of hospices, patients in some may give themselves medication, including narcotic analgesics (pain-relievers) if appropriate. *Sheltered care homes* and *halfway houses* are institutional programs in-between hospital care and living at home. They can be run economically and handle many patients. The quality of supervision varies. Some patients who function well in these can attempt more independent living in the community.

Concerning *ambulatory (out-patient) care,* 80% is provided in private doctors' offices. In general, about 75% of all visits to a physician were made to private practices. *Hospital clinics* have traditionally been institutional "stepchildren." Historically, it has been easier for hospitals to provide emergency services than to provide clinic services, one reason being that insurance companies are more apt to reimburse emergency room services. One study showed that of visits to emergency rooms, 5% were *emergent* (requiring immediate care), 45% were *urgent* (requiring care within several hours), and 50% were *non-urgent.*

The United States has the largest number of medical *specialists* per unit population. In descending order, the largest numbers are surgical subspecialists (e.g., otolaryngologists), internal medicine subspecialists (e.g., cardiologists), general practitioners, general internists and general surgeons. It should be noted, though, that many specialists (including psychiatrists) perform primary care functions. According to the 1980 *Graduate Medical Education National Advisory Committee (G.M.E.N.A.C.)* report, in 1990 the only physician shortages will be in psychiatry, emergency medicine, preventive and environmental medicine, and child psychiatry. G.M.E.N.A.C. anticipated an oversupply of practitioners of all other branches of medicine. This is ironic because in the late 1960s and early 70s, we perceived a major national undersupply of physicians, built many new medical schools, and enlarged the sizes of many existing medical school classes. This is also anxiety-producing to many medical students, who until recently had almost unlimited access to training in subspecialties they preferred. Most Western European countries are also perceiving an oversupply of physicians and are limiting the sizes of their medical school classes.

Unfortunately, economic forecasting is an inexact process, and recently some medical economists question whether there will be a physician oversupply between 1990 and 2000, and others who predict another physician shortage between 2010 and 2030.

As of 1978, about 60% of all active physicians were in office practice, and about 15% were *housestaff* (residents and interns). Although solo practice and partnership remain very common, progressively more physicians are becoming salaried employees of HMOs, group practices, and hospitals. Physicians work longer hours when they are in private practice compared to when they are salaried.

With every new technological development in medicine, new occupations are created. Thus, the greatest recent increases in the numbers of health care providers have been for *"allied health workers."* There are 12 allied health workers for every American physician. The majority of health care workers are women, but most independent practitioners such as doctors and dentists, and most health administrators, are men.

Chapter 4:

PSYCHOANALYTIC THEORY

I. TOPOGRAPHY OF THE "MIND"

The conscious is what one is aware of at a given point in time. The *preconscious* is what is accessible by a simple act of will or memory; for example, "What's the name of that Mary Tyler Moore movie that took place in Lake Forest? It's at the tip of my tongue . . . It's . . . *Ordinary People!*" Existence of the *unconscious* is inferred.

II. STRUCTURE OF THE "MIND"

The *id* is the reservoir of the infantile sexual and aggressive drives and is entirely unconscious. The *superego* is an internalized sense of right and wrong, akin to conscience, and has unconscious, preconscious and conscious components. The *ego ideal* is one's internalized ideal, basically what one ought to be like. It, too, has unconscious, preconscious and conscious components.

The *ego* is defined by what it does: this includes motor and sensory functions, intellect, reality perception and reality testing. Reality perception is the ability to correctly perceive external stimuli. The abnormalities of reality perception are hallucinations and illusions. In hallucinations, you perceive stimuli which aren't there (e.g., a Viet Nam combat veteran sees a "film" of a Viet Nam battle while walking in the woods). Reality testing is the capacity to know that a given misperception isn't a real occurrence (e.g., "That was just a 'flashback' from 'Nam! I know I'm not there.") Ego functions also include object relations (relations with others), impulse control (self-control), affectivity (the capacity to experience and convey feelings in general), and moods (our feelings at one point in time, e.g., "I feel very depressed today."). Affectivity has been likened to the climate, and moods to the weather. The ego also has an executive function of mediating among the other psychic structures and between these structures and the outside world. The ego has unconscious, preconscious and conscious components.

III. EGO DEFENSE MECHANISMS

These are defenses against anxiety. *Rationalization* is giving an acceptable explanation which isn't the basic, underlying reason. *Fixation* is partially remaining at a more childish level of development. It can be the product of excessive or insufficient parental supplying of the child's needs. *Regression* is a return to an earlier stage of functioning, which can be normal (*regression in the service of the ego*) during hospitalization and vacations. Regression is probably the most common defense mechanism experienced early in the course of people's hospitalizations. It often occurs during stressful situations such as when a child is hungry or tired or with an unfamiliar person.

Reaction formation is taking an attitude which is the opposite of an unacceptable unconscious feeling, and is seen in obsessive-compulsive neurosis and mania. *Projection* is attributing one's unwanted feelings to others; it is common in "paranoid" conditions. *Denial* is nonrecognition and nonacceptance of what should be very obvious. It is a primitive defense seen in "psychoses," upon learning of a loved one's death, and with dysfunction of the right parietal lobe of the brain.

Doing and undoing is symbolically experiencing and counteracting an unacceptable unconscious wish. For example, a person unconsciously wanting to burn down his house may compulsively check on the gas jets of his stove by turning them on and off. It is very common in obsessive-compulsive neuroses. *Repression* is the unconscious relegation of an unacceptable thought into the unconscious, and is important in many "neuroses." *Suppression* is the conscious, willful, relegation of an unwanted thought into the unconscious. *Identification* is the process of becoming

Like Someone else

coming like someone else. It is a component of (as well as sometimes caused by) *empathy,* which means putting oneself in another's position (in contrast to *sympathy,* which is feeling sorry for
another person). Identification often results from role modeling.
Ego splitting is perceiving other individuals as either all good or
all bad, rather than as complex people with strengths and short-
comings. *Displacement* is the experience of a thought and its ac-
companying mood state directed at one person when the
thought was originally directed, but unacceptably so, at another
person.

Somatization is the translation of thoughts and feelings into
"physical", "bodily," "systemic" experiences. It is common in
conversion disorder, Briquet's syndrome and hypochondriasis.
In *passive aggressivity,* one's rageful feelings are translated into
passive resistances such as being late, botching a project, or for-
getting an assignment. In *dissociation,* part of the patient's
"mind" is operating separately from the rest of it, as in *fugue
states* (where a person finds himself with another identity in another town, with no recollection of the first identity), *multiple
personality* (where a person manifests very different personalities
at different times, each personality not fully aware of the other,
as in *Three Faces of Eve* or *Dr. Jekyll and Mr. Hyde*), and psychomotor epilepsy. Fugue states and multiple personality are uncommon and are usually seen simultaneously with other disorders,
some of them serious. There is some question about the validity
of "fugue state" as a diagnosis.

Altruism is acting selflessly in dealing with others. It, and intellectualization, are reasonably developed and common in adolescence. *Intellectualization* is presenting basic, primitive ideas in a
complex, abstract fashion, (e.g., "I'm most perplexed at the
inconsistencies in your attendance and overall performance, and
we need to seek a solution to this complex problem" instead of
"I'm very ticked off at you and I'd like to fire you or kill you.")
It is seen in obsessive-compulsive disorder and psychomotor epilepsy. Like altruism, *sublimation* is a relatively mature defense. It
is defined as channeling unacceptable unconscious wishes into
socially acceptable behaviors.

A recent study suggests that *regression* is more prevalent
among suicidal psychiatric patients than among non-suicidal patients, and that displacement and denial are more common

in Violent pt >

among patients acting violently towards others than among non-violent patients.

IV. APPLICATIONS TO GENERAL MEDICAL PRACTICE

Theories of psychoanalytic therapy may apply to general medicine as well as psychiatry. For example, during a generalist's counseling sessions, patients may be encouraged to briefly *free associate*, i.e., talk about whatever comes to mind, regardless of what it is or who it's about. The patient may develop *transference reactions*, which are feelings towards the doctor that he originally held towards important figures in his life, especially his parents. These feelings could be positive, negative or *ambivalent*. The latter is what you feel when your worst enemy drives off a cliff in your Jaguar. The regression of severe illness or hospitalization fosters the transference reaction. The physician must try to be aware of his own *countertransference* feelings, which are feelings towards the patient that originated in feelings towards important people in his own (the doctor's) life. The doctor-patient relationship is highly *cathectic*, which means a great deal of psychic energy is associated with it. Occasionally, the patient will present *dreams* to the physician, which may serve as clues to problems in the doctor-patient relationship, subjects for discussion, or revelations about strong emotions that the patient is experiencing but not consciously expressing.

Chapter 5:

Habituation
Sensitization

CONDITIONING

Conditioning is how we learn and maintain new behaviors, and discontinue old behaviors. Two simple types of conditioning are habituation (first described by Dr. Ivan Pavlov) and sensitization, which are well-summarized by Dr. Eric Kandel in his text *Principles of Neural Science*. Habituation and sensitization are simple because they involve only one stimulus rather than paired stimuli. Habituation is the decrease in a reflex response to a repeated, relatively tolerable stimulus. For example, city dwellers learn not to respond with a startle to auto horns and construction sounds. In sensitization, there is an increased reflex response to relatively mild variants of a stimulus (e.g., a touch) after previous exposure to more noxious or intense forms (e.g., a slap) of the stimulus. *Classic:* *1st Stim 2nd Reflex*

Stim precedes behavior In classic (Pavlovian, after Dr. Ivan Pavlov) conditioning, behavior is *elicited* in response to a stimulus which *precedes it.* This is usually associated with *reflexive responses.* For example, when meat is presented to a dog he salivates. When a bell is paired with the meat, eventually the bell elicits salivation in the absence of the meat. *1st Reflex 2nd Stim*

In operant conditioning, behavior is *emitted* in anticipation of an event called a *reinforcer* (or reinforcing stimulus) which follows the behavior. For example, many medical school faculty work hard to help their students to learn, to publish papers, and to obtain grants.

The rest of this section will emphasize operant conditioning. In *positive reinforcement,* something needed or desired is given; for example, a child receives praise and a lollipop from the pediatrician after an examination. In *negative reinforcement,* an *aversive* stimulus is removed when the desired behavior occurs. For example, visits to a physician are reinforced when the physician removes cerumen (which impaired hearing) from the patient's ears. In *punishment,* an aversive stimulus is presented, or a desirable stimulus is not presented.

The *law of magnitude* is that the stronger the stimulus, the more likely that the behavior will occur; for example, more people will go to the doctor for severe nausea than for mild nausea. The *law of recency* is that the more closely in time a behavior is followed by a reinforcing (or punishing) stimulus, the more likely that behavior will be learned (or extinguished); for example, in teaching interviewing technique it is best to give students feedback immediately after they interview. The *law of contingency* holds that a behavior to be shaped is most likely to be learned when the person can connect that behavior to the consequent stimulus. If procaine penicillin works every time for his patients' diplococcal pneumonias (lung infections caused by a circular bacterium that lives in pairs), the physician is more likely to prescribe it for diplococcal pneumonia. The *law of effect* is that any behavior followed by a positive consequence (reward) is most apt to be repeated and any behavior followed by an aversive consequence is less likely to be repeated.

There are four basic *schedules* of reinforcement: In *fixed-ratio* schedules, rewards are given when we perform a behavior a specific number of times, such as a dermatologist receiving a fee for each visit. The latter is an example of a 1:1 ratio (called *continuous reinforcement*) schedule. In a *variable ratio* schedule, varying frequencies of behaviors (sometimes the frequencies required are unknown to the person being influenced) must occur before rewards are presented. For example, the first reward may be presented after six instances of a behavior, the second reward after three instances, and the third after 22 instances. This is a very potent system—witness the "magnetism" of "one-armed bandits" in Las Vegas. In the *fixed interval* schedule, the reward (e.g., a paycheck) is presented after a predictable time (e.g., bimonthly) has elapsed. In the *variable interval schedule,* variable, unpredictable periods of time elapse before rewards are given. One example is a doctor trying to reach a hard-to-find relative of a patient by phone.

Extinction occurs when a behavior's frequency diminishes as rewards for it cease. For example, many children's temper tantrums can be extinguished if the parents pay no attention (attention being a strong positive reinforcer) to the child during the tantrum. Some learning occurs when we watch someone else perform a rewarding activity. One example of this *modeling* process is when a medical student copies an attending physician's interviewing style and is rewarded for it.

In operant conditioning, behaviors are emitted before, and in anticipation of, a reinforcing stimulus. Preceding or at the time of the emission of the operant behavior, a *discriminative stimulus* is often present. This is a stimulus which does not elicit the behavior by itself, but will increase the likelihood of the behavior occurring. This takes place when the discriminative stimulus was previously present in circumstances where the desired behavior was reinforced. For example, a doctor's office is a discriminative stimulus which increases the likelihood of a patient presenting a thoughtful history (the desired behavior) to the doctor that the patient wouldn't present to the doctor if he ran into the doctor at a baseball game.

We learn not only to identify stimuli; we also begin to *distinguish among* gradations and variations of the stimuli. This is called the development of *discriminative capacity*. For example, early in a medical student's career he will learn to identify a hand tremor (rhythmic contractions of the hand or fingers) and be rewarded for it; later, he will distinguish among types of hand tremors.

Also, we learn to overlook distinctions between cues that resemble each other in order to predict forthcoming rewards or punishments. For example, a child that has had to take unpleasant-tasting medication from a bottle may later refuse to take a pleasant-tasting medication from a similar bottle. In contrast to the above example, *generalization learning* can also be adaptive. An example of *stimulus generalization* that is potentially helpful is the *transference* reaction in psychotherapy, where the patient emits responses towards the therapist in anticipation of reinforcements like those he received from his parents.

We learn not only to emit a behavior, but we also can learn to produce it in a specific way. *Topography* refers to the gradations and varieties of the behavior performed, a step beyond simply whether the behavior occurs. For example, at the beginning of a Little League season a child learns to hit a pitched ball; after several seasons he can position his body to hit the ball to either side of the baseball diamond.

To learn a behavior, the individual must be motivated to learn it, and this is largely determined by the nature and timing of the reinforcement which follows. *Supraordinate stimuli* inform the person of those aspects of a stimulus to which he should pay attention. For humans, words are probably the most common supraordinate stimuli. For example, in teaching auscultation (listening with the stethoscope) of the left anterior chest, the instructor will say "Listen for 'whooshing' sounds. These sounds are called murmurs." This will increase the chances of the student emitting the desired behavior, auscultation of (listening to) the chest for murmurs, which will be reinforced when he hears a murmur and this is confirmed by the instructor with praise.

Chapter 6:

CHILD DEVELOPMENT

Child development is best presented age-group by age-group:

I. INFANCY (Birth to 1 1/2) *Oral period ; Id*

Psychoanalysts call this the *oral period,* where the primary *erotogenic* (pleasure-giving) *zone* is the mouth, pharynx, buccal mucosa and lips. Rephrased, the oral area is highly *cathectic,* meaning that great amounts of psychic energy are associated with it. The *id* predominates. The sub-phase of *primary narcissism* (whereby the infant is unable to perceive individual people, viewing the world as amorphous) begins this period. The only ego present during the oral phase is the *conflict-free sphere* of ego which encompasses motor and sensory functions.

Later in the oral phase, Dr. Rene Spitz' *ego organizers* (stages in the individuation of objects in the environment) appear. At approximately three months, the infant manifests the *social smile* (3) which is an automatic smile upon seeing the eyes, nose and mouth of a face (or face mask). At around 6 months there is (6) *stranger anxiety,* whereby the infant cries automatically in the company of an unfamiliar person. Stranger anxiety will not occur, however, unless there is an initial *bonding (attachment)* with a parent. At about 18 months, there is *negative head shaking:* the child shakes his head "no" to almost everything, even things he likes. This represents the autonomous position, "I have a mind of my own," which is a harbinger of the anal period to be discussed later.

At about one year of age, most children start using *transitional objects,* which are favorite items (e.g., a Linus blanket) that children use as substitutes for parental supports when parents are absent. Parent-child bonding is critical to normal development and affects later child-parent interactions. It begins within the first several weeks of life, and is manifested by visual tracking of objects, responding to stimuli from people, and moving along with the rhythms of words. Negative effects on bonding occur when a child has an illness or deformity, is premature or of low birth weight, or is separated from the parents. At this stage of development, the crucial factors for child-rearing are contact and comfort and affectionate time. Discipline, absence of hypocrisy, and positive reinforcement are less important in infancy. According to Dr. Erik Erikson, infancy is also the time during which *basic trust* develops. For the child's basic trust to develop, he must have the capacity for *object permanence* (a concept of Dr. Jean Piaget), whereby the child senses that even if the parent figure disappears, he will return again. The game peek-a-boo reinforces object permanence.

The newborn child manifests many primitive reflexes: He automatically grasps at a finger placed in the palm of his hand, turns his head in the direction of stroking on his cheek *(rooting reflex),* sucks on a finger placed in his mouth, makes stepping movements with his legs when he is held upright, and manifests a *Babinski reflex.* In the latter, the great toe extends upward when the inferolateral aspect of that foot is stroked. He breathes irregularly, sleeps a lot (half of his sleep is REM sleep), and is capable of some conditioning. Survival of the newborn is statistically related to maternal height, maternal age, maternal mental status and the number of other children in the home. Socioeconomic status differences manifest themselves even in early infancy.

On the average, the following occur: at 5 months the child can roll over; at 7 months he can sit unsupported; at 10 months he can feed himself; at one year, he can stand and speak his first word; at 15 months he can walk and build a tower of two cubes; and at 18 months he can throw a ball and is aware of anatomic sex differences. His *gender identity* (whether he/she thinks he is a boy or girl) is largely the gender that parents "assign" him, so if an infant boy is routinely told he is a girl, he will think he is one.

Recent research suggests that *empathy* may begin late in infancy, as in the case of a 15-month-old who offered his teddy bear to a crying friend. Regarding *birth order,* first-born children are more apt to be bright, successful and ambitious. Among psychiatrists, there is a disproportionately large number of first-borns. Many factors could be at play here, including better maternal and paternal health, more time for parents to expend, higher parental expectations, and more opportunities to take a leadership role.

Problem areas in infancy include the following:

Prematurity and *low birth weight* are the biological factors most frequently correlated with *mental retardation,* which is more common in boys than in girls. For the vast majority of the mentally retarded, the cause is unknown. Causes can include single or multiple genes, defective chromosomes, pseudoretardation due to deafness, or an artefact of poorly-conducted I.Q. testing. *Down's syndrome* (trisomy 21, Mongolism) is a common known cause of retardation. It can occur with 46 *(translocation Down's)* or 47 chromosomes, and is more likely to occur with older maternal or paternal age.

Tay-Sachs disease (Type 1) appears at about 6 months of age. It is due to an autosomal recessive abnormality of the *long arm of chromosome 15,* which leads to a deficiency of the enzyme B-d-N hexosaminidase with the consequent deposition of a gangloside (a phosphorus-free fat containing sugar) in the brain (causing retardation), the retina (leading to blindness & revealing a *"cherry-red spot"* on the macula seen on ophthalmoscopy). As of 1988, it is fatal, but some day perhaps the normal enzyme will be genetically manufactured and transported across the blood-brain barrier. It is an uncommon disease seen most often in Eastern European Jews.

Lesch-Nyhan syndrome appears at about age 1, and is rare. It is transmitted recessively on the *long arm* of the *x chromosome,* leading to decreased activity of the enzyme hypoxanthine-guanine phosphoribyl transferase (HGPRT), causing disturbed purine metabolism with *increased blood uric acid.* The severity of mental retardation is variable. At age 1, *choreoathetoid* (jerky and writhing) *movements,* and speech impediments, appear. The most salient feature is *self-mutilating behavior* from which the children feel pain, and when they are old enough to talk will plead with others to keep them from biting themselves. As of 1990, we cannot successfully treat this illness. However, the normal HGPRT gene has been successfully *cloned* (isolated from a large DNA mixture), and some day, this gene or its product HGPRT may be transported across the blood-brain barrier.

Dr. Leo Kanner described a severe chronic syndrome called *early infantile autism,* which, like mental retardation, is more common in boys. The autistic child shows virtually no interpersonal relatedness with parents or siblings or other children; for example, unlike most children he does not position himself in anticipation of being picked up. The prevalence is about 2.5/100,000 children. The child manifests decreased intelligence, and is mute or has a formal thinking disorder. Frequent twirling, rocking, headbanging or other agitated or stereotyped behaviors are common. The prognosis is poor, with approximately half remaining mute and half (not necessarily the ones who are mute) requiring permanent institutionalization. It used to be thought that the typical parents of an autistic child were cold, aloof and overly intellectual, but we no longer believe this to be the case.

Another cause of mental retardation is *protein deficiency,* sometimes called *kwarshiorkor,* which manifests diminished growth, abdominal protuberance and apathy. In the laboratory, the serum protein level is usually decreased. *Fetal alcohol syndrome* is also associated with mental retardation. The children are usually short and low in weight and have certain facial characteristics involving the eyes, nose, maxilla and mouth.

Another severe problem of infancy, fortunately rare in its advanced form, is what Dr. Rene Spitz termed *anaclitic depression.* Dr. Spitz observed this severe *maternal deprivation syndrome* in a prison nursery in 6–8 month old infants whose mothers became unavailable for significant periods of time. They manifested crying, weight loss, insomnia, apathy, impaired development, and susceptibility to infection. After three months it became irreversible, and death due to *marasmus* (extreme emaciation with "wasting" of body tissues) occurred after two years.

Regarding *parental unavailability or death,* Dr. John Bowlby described a progression of *mourning* behaviors in children (as well as nonhuman primate children) which went from protest to despair to apathy. This progression is seen in *hospitalized* children. To minimize its intensity, prehospital visits, prehospital discussions with play rehearsal, frequent visits or live-in situations for parents, and bringing of favorite toys or objects (e.g., transitional objects) to the hospital, are all helpful. The hospitalization should be discussed truthfully in terms the child can understand; for example, if the child is expected to experience some pain, this should probably be discussed.

Another problem area of infancy we will discuss is *child abuse,* which is not confined to infancy, but is most commonly suffered by children under 5, who can't readily escape, complain, or fight back. Often, child abuse is first identified in emergency rooms, where it is suspected if the child has multiple injuries, or multiple visits due to traumatic injury. Child abuse sometimes occurs in children who don't live up to their parents' expectations or gratify their parents' dependency needs, or who are scapegoated, premature or unplanned. In perhaps half the cases, the abusing parent was himself abused. In many cases, the parent is immature or a drug user who does not foster a strong parent-child bond by meeting the child's needs, even though he may make a good initial impression and attribute the family's problems to others.

The *scapegoating* of a child may result from displacing hostility onto the child during a marital problem, and in turn may increase family friction and lead to self-fulfilling prophecies.

Prematurity is a common theme in much childhood (and probably also adulthood) psychopathology. It is more common when the parent is single, poor, a young teenager, a substance abuser or a smoker. The child is more likely to be scapegoated and abused and to fail to thrive, and is less likely to be held and given sufficient attention by parents. His parents are more likely to feel distant from him. *Failure to thrive* is a "final common pathway," subacute or chronic, of systemic medical conditions (e.g., ear or urinary infections) or deprivations. Failure to thrive manifests itself as delayed growth and development and irritability or apathy.

II. TODDLERHOOD (AGES 1-1/2-3) *Anal*

Psychoanalysts call this the *anal period* of psychosexual development, whereby the anus, rectum, buttocks and perineal region are the most highly cathectic. *Toilet training*, with its theme of self-control and autonomy versus external control, is a milestone. Improved motor skills, continued development of gender identity (which is established by 2 1/2), and acquisition of some *autonomy*, take place here. The *normal negativism* represented by negative head shaking ushers in this period. The child still has trouble sharing his parents' attention with others.

In this stage, developing motor skills outstrip judgment, so *accidents* due to the child "getting into things (e.g., taking medicine from a cabinet)" may occur. On the average, at two years the child can run and speak in two word sentences. On the average, at three he can ride a tricycle, put on shoes without tying the laces, speak in fluent sentences, and copy a circle.

As motor activity exceeds judgment, *accidental poisoning* is most common during this period. Some correlates of accidental poisoning include previous poisoning, stimulus-bound hyperactivity and low socioeconomic status. Other than in the pathologic syndrome called *pica,* where the child recurrently ingests non-nutritive substances such as chipped lead-containing paint with its consequent risk of *lead poisoning,* fixation at a stage of "orality" has never been proven to cause accidental poisoning.

Another subject that may need discussion during this period is *adoption.* Adopted children are more likely to have behavior problems than their non-adopted counterparts. The reasons are not well understood, and might include genetic and prenatal health factors, diminished self esteem surrounding knowledge of being adopted, and preference by some family members for biological relatives. It is important to discuss adoption early in the child's life, and to present it so that it can be a source of pride for the child (e.g., "We wanted to have a child very badly, and we were so happy when we got you."). Frequently, during adolescence or adulthood adopted children express a desire to meet their biologic parents. In recent years, authorities and parents have been more willing to honor this request. Many children in *foster care* (which is usually temporary) are placed multiple times.

III. THE PRESCHOOL CHILD (Ages 3-6) *Oedipal/phallic*

Psychoanalysts call this the *Oedipal/phallic period* with considerable cathexis of the genital region which becomes the primary erotogenic zone. The *Oedipus complex* is thought to occur. This is where the child falls in love with the parent of the opposite sex and wants to marry that parent and kill the same-sex parent. The child fears retaliation by that same-sex parent. The complex is resolved when the child begins to appreciate the same-sex parent as loving and nonthreatening. In conjunction with this, the *superego* simultaneously develops by the child incorporating the parents' values.

According to Dr. Erikson, major themes during this period include *initiative* and *guilt.* Initiative refers to the fact that the child enjoys taking and receiving some responsibility. Guilt can occur for the first time because of the child's newly-developing conscience.

On the average, at age 4, the child can copy a plus sign (+) and throw a ball overhand. At five, he can copy a square and usually knows something of his racial or *ethnic identity*. On the average, at six he can perform some complex coordinated activities (e.g., ice skating), can copy a triangle, and can begin attending school.

During the preschool period, genital play is common. About one quarter of children have *imaginary companions*. These are usually temporary and non-pathologic and sometimes appear following a stressful event. At this stage, if a child is hospitalized, his greatest fears are of mutilation, separation and punishment. He cannot yet comprehend death's finality.

Toilet training should be complete by age 3. However, about 30–40% of children, boys more than girls, manifest *enuresis* (bedwetting), which has many causes. These include urologic disease, regression under stress, impaired stage 4 sleep, or familial/genetic factors. Treatment should depend upon the cause if found, and may include psychologic support, behavior modification, bladder retraining, urologic surgery or imipramine.

Like some cases of enuresis, most if not all cases of *night terrors (pavor nocturnus)* occur during stage 4 of sleep. Unlike nightmares, which are recallable dreams that occur during REM sleep, night terrors do not occur during or following recallable dreams. The child awakens screaming, is not readily calmed, and has no recollection of the night terror when he awakens in the morning. If frequent and distressing, it can be treated with benzodiazepines, which suppress stage 4 sleep.

IV. THE SCHOOL AGE CHILD (7–10)

Psychoanalysts call this period *latency*, whereby there is (due in part to the influence of parents and teachers) considerable repression of earlier sexuality and sublimation of this sexuality into curiosity, playing with same-sex chums, and industriousness. The superego, initially developed during the Oedipal period, develops further but is rather rigid.

The child can adhere to rules (often rigidly) in playing games, may steal once or twice, and begins to understand the concepts (first described by Dr. Piaget) of *conservation* (e.g., water poured from a short, wide glass into a tall, narrow glass stays the same in quantity) and *reversibility* (If 3 + 8 equals 11, 11 minus 8 equals 3). On the average, at age 7 he can copy a diamond, and at 8 he can perceive death as permanent.

The *minimum brain dysfunction/attention deficit hyperactivity disorder* (ADHD) most commonly presents during this phase affecting 10% of boys and 2% of girls! It is not a single disease, but rather (to quote Dr. Charles Popper) a "final common pathway" for a group of conditions characterized by "stimulant-responsive impulsivity." ADHD can occur in autism, conduct disorders, affective disorders, Tourette's disorder (see p. 77) and hyperthyroidism, and can be a medication side effect. The child manifests stimulus-bound motor hyperactivity and has decreased concentration and attention span. Neurologic *soft signs* are common. These are signs that suggest brain dysfunction but which cannot routinely be localized within the brain; an example is the *grasp reflex,* where the child automatically grasps the examiner's finger placed in the palm of the child's hand. Also common are neuropsychologic test abnormalities and nonspecific electroencephalographic abnormalities. It is more common in the U.S. than elsewhere, it runs in families; it is more common in children of low birth weight or with severe early childhood malnutrition. On average, they have higher blood lead levels than do their siblings. The first treatment of choice is stimulant medication. In one hypothesis about this disorder, there is deficient monoamine production in certain parts of the brain.

The most common adult outcome of ADHD is normality, but it can persist into adulthood, and can be a precurser of other syndromes, such as sociopathy (which occurs in 25% of cases of ADHD and which is associated with adult criminality.

School phobia also commonly occurs during this time. The child fears going to school and avoids it at all costs. Symptoms often diminish on weekends. It frequently presents in pediatricians' or generalists' offices with somatic complaints. It is thought by some to result from problems in separation and developing autonomy from the parents, and that it might be prevented by fostering the development of autonomy. It can be triggered with a stressful event. Treatment begins with the child being sent to school.

Children of this and other ages are exposed to considerable *televised violence,* the effect of which has been studied. This viewing is correlated with increases in aggressive behavior, diminished sensitivity to subsequent media violence, increased likelihood of viewing violence as a means of solving problems, learning new ways of being aggressive, and having a greater likelihood of producing violent content on projective psychological testing (standardized testing such as the Rorschach ink blots in which the patient is asked to respond to ambiguous stimuli).

Mild mental retardation is usually identified for the first time during this period. Mildly retarded children need special education and vocational training programs. Some cases of psychosis occur during this period.

Specific developmental disorders are impairments of individual academic skills compared with the child's overall IQ, which is often normal or even superior. All are familial; all but one are more common in boys. Autosomal dominant transmission of an abnormality of *chromosome 15* is responsible for some cases of *developmental reading disorder* (common dyslexia).

V. ADOLESCENCE

Defined sometimes as the transition between childhood and adulthood, it begins with the physiologic changes of *puberty*. The approximate age range is 11–20, but is thought to be prolonged beyond 20 in middle class urbanized cultures with extended dependency due to schooling. During adolescence there is a reawakening of earlier libidinal feelings, improvement of self-control, major strides in autonomy, finalization of *sex object preference*, clarification of body image and major development of *identity*. Identity is a sense of sameness and continuity over time. Adolescence is often a time of *identity crises* (e.g., "Who am I?", "What do I want from life?"), which are handled in part by discussions of occupational goals, starting relationships with adults besides one's parents, understanding one's sexual desires, and cultivating one's altruism. Parents need to be very supportive and only mildly to moderately controlling. Discipline is very important, however.

Almost all teenage boys, and most teenage girls, masturbate. Cognitively, there is for the first time a capacity for advanced, logical, abstract thinking with the ability to deal in symbols and the idea of causality. This is Piaget's stage of *formal operations*.

Between 5 and 18, people have the fewest doctor visits. The most common cause of death, and one of the most common causes of doctor visits, is *accidents*. Possibly many accidents could be prevented by anticipatory discussions. *Homicide* and *suicide* are the second and third leading causes of death in teenagers. Regarding *suicide* by teenagers, drug overdose is the most common vehicle for attempts. The commonest diagnosis associated with suicide is depression. In an adolescent, depression can present as apathy, social withdrawal, worsening of grades, and substance abuse, as well as classic depressive symptoms and signs like a sad or anxious mood, loss of appetite and weight, and severe guilt feelings. There is some preliminary evidence that television reports of people committing suicide influence some susceptible teenagers to kill themselves. This supports the popular belief that teenagers are more susceptible to fads and fashions than are adults.

Although the mean age of onset for schizophrenia, mania and endogenous depression is beyond 20, many cases start in teen years. Drug abuse is very common among teenagers. In general, almost all adult psychiatric disorders can begin in childhood.

It may surprise you to learn that *incest* occurs frequently enough to be a significant national problem. The exact incidence is unknown because most cases aren't reported to authorities, and because the problem is not readily identified by professionals. Father-daughter incest is more common than mother-son incest. It is believed that often the mother is openly or secretly aware of the incest, but doesn't take any dramatic action because she feels it would disrupt the family life and "psychic equilibrium." The parents often have problems in their sexual and other personal relationships. The long-term effect of incest is not yet well known.

Many teenagers, girls more than boys, *run away* from home. Often, there is some problem in the family (e.g., an abusive alcoholic parent) which is intolerable to the teenager. Most runaways eventually return home. Runaways have an increased prevalence of depression and venereal disease and adult sociopathy. There are now a number of agencies that help runaways.

Probably most latency-age or teenage children steal something, just for the excitement and to see if they can get away with it. Out of context, the meaning of an act of *shoplifting* is impossible to determine, as it could represent anything from a "normal" behavior to an early sign of sociopathy.

Many teenagers marry and get pregnant—not necessarily both, and not necessarily in that order. *Teenage pregnancies* have increased medical risks, in part because of a tendency for them to take poorer care of themselves prenatally, which includes seeking less prenatal medical care. Teenage pregnancies are predictive of future teenage pregnancies, increased risk of divorce, and school dropout. The earlier the first pregnancy, the lower the future income and the greater the risk of eventually being on welfare.

Some cases of *mild mental retardation*, such as in *Klinefelter's syndrome*, may first be diagnosed during adolescence. The teenage boy with Klinefelter's manifests tall stature, small testes, sparse pubic hair, and feminine breast tissue development. Sex chromosome makeup is XXY, XXXY, etc. The more Xs, the greater the chance of retardation or severe retardation.

Wilson's disease is rare, can appear as early as age 4 and as late as 50, with the mean age of onset in most countries being from 12–16, and in the U.S. at 23, suggesting an influence of nongenetic variables. The autosomal recessive defect is on the *long arm of chromosome 13*, leading to impaired biliary excretion of copper that in turn leads to accumulations of copper in the liver (causing *cirrhosis*, characterized by deposition of fat, hypertrophy of connective tissue, and overall degeneration and deformity), the cornea of the eye (causing a golden-brown or greenish discoloration called a *Kayser-Fleischer ring*, and brain (leading to dementia with prominent frontal lobe features [see p. 90] and seizures). (For the sake of semantic clarity, dementias of childhood and adolescence are labelled as retardation.) Treatment includes *D-penicillamine*, which binds copper and enhances urinary excretion, and a low-copper diet.

Chapter 7:

GENDER-RELATED PSYCHOLOGY

During the past decade, there has been increased interest in the similarities and differences in the behavior (innate and learned) of women and men. A sizable literature has emerged on common problems of women.

One major stumbling block in this area is the difficulty in separating gender-related differences due to biology, culture, and research bias. Differences in behavior between boy and girl neonates (newborn to one month old) haven't been demonstrated. Maccoby and Jacklin's review supports a statistical conclusion that after age 11, girls have more *verbal ability* and after 12 or 13, boys have more *visual-spatial* and *mathematical* ability. Across all societies, males are more *aggressive* than females. Aggressivity can be experimentally increased in some animal species by administering testosterone. After conception, at all ages females are more apt to survive than males.

Among women who socialize a great deal together (regardless of whether they are relatives), there is a tendency for the times of their menstruation to come closer together. McClintock identified this phenomenon among students in a college dormitory, and labelled it *menstrual synchrony*. At menopause, there are systemic vasomotor changes which result in "hot flashes," and vaginal mucosal thinning.

Women make more annual *visits to physicians*, and were more apt to be taken to physicians as children. A major contributing factor may be an expectation that men should "tough it out" when they are troubled, ill, or injured. Mental disorders in general are more apt to be diagnosed in women (the word hysterical come from "hysteros," the Greek word for uterus), although many of the more serious and less curable disorders (e.g., schizophrenia, sociopathy and alcoholism) are more common in men.

Abortion and rape are, appropriately, subjects of intense political and medicolegal interest. *Abortion* is sought by women of all socioeconomic levels. Whether a physician performs abortions is largely a product of his/her personal beliefs, apart from his technical skill and local laws. Abortion is a relatively safe medical procedure in the first trimester. Most abortions are not followed by clinically significant depression. In fact, the majority of women experience a preponderance of relief compared to negative psychological consequences.

Most *rapes* are planned and intraracial, and 50% of rapists are intoxicated when they commit this crime. Many rapists know their victims. There is a developing literature that rape victims have psychological sequelae, but not necessarily major psychiatric illness.

Taking a *sexual history* should be handled as any other section of the interview. As long as questions are relevant to the patient's care, and are asked nonvoyeuristically, nonjudgmentally and tactfully, a detailed sexual history usually can be obtained in a straightforward, matter-of-fact fashion.

Concerning occupational factors, women comprise about 40% of the paid labor force. They are more apt to get *lower-paying, lower-status jobs*. Perhaps for the above reason, or as a result of child-rearing, women have greater job absenteeism than do men.

Chapter 8:

AGING, DYING AND DEATH

I. THE AGED

This is the fastest-growing age group in the population. There are now about 23,000,000 people over 65, about 10% of the population. By the year 2030, the aged will comprise about 20% of the population. This results partly from the increasing American life expectancy, though the life span itself is not expanding.

The aged have many *social problems:* They are *poorer* than other groups, with only 25% in the labor force. Pensions are usually fixed incomes vulnerable to inflation. Many of the elderly are agricultural workers, and many cannot afford telephones. They constitute 10% of the total population, but 20% of the poor.

They are *more isolated* because of disability, spousal death and death of friends, a greater chance of being hospitalized when ill, greater geographic mobility in recent decades, a decline of the extended family, and their lesser acceptance of psychiatric treatment. Their *status* is comparatively lower. They are less well schooled, and have often been replaced by vocational schools for vocational tutoring of the young. Also, our culture emphasizes the future over the present and past. They are often seen as less attractive and less valuable, and are often the victim of stereotypes formed by people with minimal exposure to them.

They are *medically-underserved,* receiving fewer consultations for the same illnesses, with cognitive dysfunctions often missed, physician underestimation of the prognosis of their diseases, few specialists in geriatric medicine (many find it a depressing spe-

cialty) and psychiatry, and underemphasis on primary prevention and overemphasis on maintenance. In one recent study,
only 50/120 medical schools formally taught about aging.

Physiologically, there is greater variability among the elderly
than among the young. They are more susceptible to *drug reactions* and therefore require lower doses. They have only 10% of
the *immune capacity* of an adolescent. They can enjoy sex, with
the best predictor of sexual frequency and enjoyment being pre-
aging frequency and enjoyment. There is a delaying of ejaculation. However, with aging, there is a decrease in the *frequency of
sex,* a decrease in the volume of ejaculate and of vaginal lubrication, and shortening in length and width of the vaginal barrel,
and thinning of vaginal barrel mucosa. There is loss of height
and subcutaneous tissue, diminished taste and smell, impaired
dentition, decreased *fluid intelligence* (problem-solving ability
with new information), EEG slowing in the alpha, delta and
theta frequencies, diminished serum estrogen levels, increased
brain monoamine oxidase (an enzyme that breaks down certain
catecholamines), increased plasma norepinephrine in response
to stress, *increased frequency of psychiatric illness* (with depression
and dementia most common), and (not surprisingly) the *highest
suicide rates* of any age group. Declines in intellect are often related to problems of systemic health, such as increase in blood
pressure and treatment for it.

However, *crystallized intelligence* (fund of information) improves
to age 50 and often holds steady after that, and some individuals
maintain cognitive excellence or brilliance. First episodes of *mania* in the elderly are less severe than for the young, and are
associated with fewer recurrences. In general, diseases curable
in the young are curable in the elderly. Results of *psychotherapy* in
the elderly can be excellent because many of the elderly perceive
themselves as having little time to waste. In doing psychotherapy or providing other medical care for the elderly, physicians
should usually address the patients by a title (e.g., Mr. Jones,
vs. "John," the latter which can appear demeaning), be willing
to touch them, and to accept periods of silence. Most of this
(exception: teenagers like being called by first names) also applies to the psychotherapy of younger patients. *Stability of the
environment* is important to the elderly; moving an elderly person
to more modern facilities, or hospitalizing him, can worsen his
mental status and overall health.

One of the more common severe syndromes in the elderly is
Alzheimer's disease, synonyms for which are senile brain disease
and primary degenerative dementia. An estimated 2.5 million

Americans have this illness. It is more common in women and accounts for the majority of the 5% of our aged population with dementia. About a third of people dying beyond age 80 show some pathologic signs of it. The degree of intellectual impairment is positively and significantly correlated with the number of senile plaques found in the brain. Alzheimer's disease is associated with Down's syndrome and leukemia (malignant overproduction of white blood cells) in some families. In 20–30% of families there appears to be autosomal dominant transmission of the condition. A gene on chromosome 21 was recently found to be responsible for the abnormal deposits in the brain that characterize Alzheimer's disease. Although Alzheimer's disease is to date incurable, a preliminary study showed that the drug tetrahydroaminoacridine can improve a patient's performance of some routine activities of his daily living, such as feeding himself, doing housework, and performing at work.

II. DYING AND DEATH

Before the 1960s, death simply meant cessation of life functions and was "diagnosed" by inspection for movement, assessment of pupillary light reflexes, palpation for pulses, and auscultation (listening) for heart sounds. Now there are two "types" of death. *Somatic death* refers to the above description. *Brain death* occurs when the heart and kidneys are still working, the lungs are being mechanically aerated, and the brain is totally nonfunctional, with somatic death virtually certain in 3 months. *Harvard Criteria for brain death* are unresponsivity, no movement or breathing, no reflexes, and a *flat* (straight line with no waves) *EEG* (see p. 60).

In 1969, Kubler-Ross described normal behaviors of dying patients and their families: *denial* (see p. 37), *anger* (e.g., at oneself for imperfect self-care, or doctors for failure to promptly diagnose and cure), *bargaining* (the posture that if one behaves well, he will somehow be rewarded), *depression* (see below), and *acceptance* (a composed coming-to-terms with death).

Regarding depression, in 1968 Clayton surveyed *bereaved* relatives of recently-deceased patients. She found that many of the mourning relatives experienced symptoms seen in clinical depressions, symptoms which usually lasted about 6 months with no medical treatment required. These symptoms included sadness, crying, anxiety attacks, sleep and concentration disturbance, and appetite and weight loss.

Chapter 9:

ELECTROENCEPHALOGRAMS (EEGs)

The electroencephalogram was invented by Dr. Hans Berger, a psychiatrist. Techniques to enhance the likelihood of obtaining seizure or other abnormal brain activity on the EEG tracing include: sleep-induction through use of hypnotic agents and *sleep deprivation; hyperventilation;* and *photic stimulation.* Wave types, moving from slowest to fastest, are delta, theta, alpha and beta. Delta is seen in deep sleep. Delta and theta are seen in foci of brain pathology, and seen diffusely in delirium. *Alpha* occurs during relaxation with diminished attentiveness and the eyes closed. *Beta* is seen during attentiveness with eyes open, and as an effect of certain medications.

Spiking, spike-and-domes, and sometimes sharp waves are seen during *seizure activity.* One exception is *6 and 14 per second positive spiking* which can be normal or seen in minimum brain dysfunction/hyperactivity/attention deficit syndrome. *Three per second spikes and domes* are seen in *petit mal epilepsy* and were reported in a patient with digitalis (a drug used in the treatment of heart failure or arrhythmia) toxicity.

Evoked potentials are electrical responses of the brain to stimuli such as sounds (*auditory evoked potentials*) or visual images (*visual evoked potentials*). Since electroencephalographers cannot identify these potentials from routine EEGs, computers are used.

Evoked potentials can help to diagnose diseases characterized by deterioration of the myelin sheath around nerve cells (such as multiple sclerosis).

Wave types (slowest to fastest)
1 - Delta   3 - Alpha
2 - theta   4 - Beta

sleepwalking
⇨ Night terrors

- Delta: seen in deep sleep (non REM) Stages 3 + 4 of sleep; Comatose
- " & theta: are seen in foci of brain pathology; & seen diffusely in delirium.
- Alpha: seen during Relaxation + attentiveness & Eyes Closed
- Beta: " during Attentiveness, Eyes Open, & certain medications
                    (antiarrhythmics)
- Spike & domes: & Sharp waves & seen during Seizures Activity
  (Exception 6 + 14/sec positive spiking can be normal or seen in
   MBD/HADS.)
      - 3/sec spikes & Domes → Pepit Mal
                                Digitalis toxicity

- K complexes: seen in Sleep-Related Periodic myoclonus

Evoked potentials:
       - Electrical Responsiveness of the Brain to
Stimuli such as Sound, Visual Images
       - help Dx Dis. character. by
       deterioration of the Myelin Sheath.
              eg Multiple Sclerosis

Chapter 10:

PSYCHOLOGICAL TESTING

There are many types of psychological test instruments, but we will cover only five categories:

I. INTELLIGENCE TESTS

Intelligence has been variously defined from the ability to solve problems by reasoning to "whatever intelligence tests measure." Most have well-demonstrated *reliability* and *validity* in predicting *school performance* and *occupational success,* and are also reasonable tests of *cognitive functioning.* Between ages 0 and 2 *developmental scales,* such as the *Denver Developmental Scale* (introduced by Frankenburg and Dodds), are used. Between 2 and 6, the *Wechsler Preschool Inventory (WPSI)* or *Stanford-Binet* (developed by Alfred Binet and modified by Dr. Lewis Terman) are used. For ages 6–12 the *Wechsler Intelligence Scale for Children-Revised (WISC-R)* is employed. For ages 13 and over, the *Wechsler Adult Intelligence Scale (WAIS)* is utilized. Based on adoption, twin and other studies, there is evidence for a major genetic causal component to I.Q. For example, the correlation between IQs of identical twins reared apart is greater than that of fraternal twins reared together. However, environment plays a key role as well. Intelligence test performance tends to be stable over the elementary, high school and college period. Nevertheless, for a given individual, this may not be the case. *Factors affecting scores* include examiner-related effects such as poor administration of the test, and subject-related effects such as genetic makeup, intrauterine influences, environmental stimulation, parental availability, amount of prior schooling, health, coaching for the test, having taken the test previously, and mood and motivation during the test.

II. PROJECTIVE TESTS

In these tests which have been used for many decades, the subject is presented with vague, *ambiguous stimuli* and asked for specific, tangible responses. These responses supposedly reflect the patient's "innermost feelings," helping the examiner to understand the patient's "psychodynamics" (which is in large part the unconscious influences on the patient's behavior and personality). In the *Rorschach* test (developed by Dr. Herman Rorschach), the stimulus is a series of standardized ink blots. In the *Thematic Apperception Test* (introduced by Dr. Henry A. Murray), the stimulus is drawings of people. In the *Sentence Completion*, (Rohde and Rotter each developed separate versions), the subject completes an incomplete sentence. In the *Word Association Test* (used for diagnostic purposes for the first time by Dr. Carl Jung), it is words to which the subject is asked to respond with the "next word which comes to mind." In the *Draw-a-Person Test,* the subject is asked to draw a picture of a person on a blank piece of paper.

III. PERSONALITY INVENTORIES

These are instruments designed to identify clusters of personality traits. The classic one is the *Minnesota Multiphasic Personality Inventory* (the *MMPI,* introduced in 1942 by Hathaway and McKinley), which is a useful research instrument. Another is Dr. Meyer Friedman and Dr. Ray Rosenman's *Type A/B Personality Scale,* which looks for a cluster of type A traits such as ambition, preoccupation with numbers and accomplishments, and having a sense of time pressure. Some, but not all, studies have shown this cluster to be associated with coronary artery disease. The *Millon Inventory* (developed by Dr. Theodore Millon) is helpful in making diagnoses according to the *Third Diagnostic and Statistical Manual of the American Psychiatric Association, Revised Edition (DSMIIIR).*

IV. TESTS FOR COARSE BRAIN DISEASE

These include the *Luria-Nebraska* (designed by Dr. Alexander Luria, with a scoring system by Dr. Charles Golden) and *Halstead-Reitan* (created by Drs. Ward Halstead and Ralph Reitan) batteries, and brief screening instruments such as the *Mini Mental State Examination* of Folstein, Folstein and McHugh, the *Reitan-Indiana Aphasia Screening Test*, and the *Bender-Gestalt* test devised by Dr. Loretta Bender using figures created by Dr. Max Wertheimer.

V. LIFE CHANGE SCALES

A synonym for life changes is life events. Regardless of whether these events are happy (e.g., the birth of a baby) or sad (e.g., the death of a parent), the sum of a person's life changes has a small positive but statistically significant correlation with his becoming ill (in any way). Life change events can be quanitified by the *Holmes-Rahe,* or other life change scales.

5-Stages of Sleep

1: fast waves; Light Sleep
2: " " ; " " (But not as fast or Light)
   45% of the Adult Sleep
3: Slow (Delta) Waves; Deep Sleep; 10% of Adult Sleep
4: Slower (") " ; Deeper Sleep
   - Night Terrors (Pavos Nocturnes) Not Remembered dreams Ex: diazepine
   mc ♂ - Sleep Walking → Asso w/ Visual Agnosia
   - Enuresis → tx Imipramine
   - ↓ Stage 4 by Benzodiazepines

5: REM sleep :- Occurs every 90 - 110 min
   - Last; beginning of sleep; few mins
                end of Night; 20 - 40 mins
   - Never starts w/normal sleep only in narcolepsy
       - Newborns
       - Congenital Blind
       - Dogs Reared in Dark
   . Asso w/ :- ↑ HR, BP, Vent
       - ↓ Muscle tone (Excep Eyes)
       - Clitoral & Penile Erection
   - Vivid Recallable dreams, & Night Mares

↓ of REM: Dx's: Alcohol, Phenothiazine, tricyclic A/dep, MAO Inhib., Barbiturates, Benzodiazepines →↓ Stage 4 — all cause Rebound REM — REM begins earliers in in sleep & last longer

2) Endogenous Depression — Shorter Latent period between REM — More REM at beginning Night-less at end — less slow wave sleep

Asso/w/REM:

SLEEP

- Narcolepsy
- Cataplexy
- Hypnogogic Hallucinations
- Night Mares

↓ reversed pattern

Many people (up to 30% in some prevalence studies) have sleep problems. Impaired sleep almost always accompanies acute psychiatric and systemic illness. Sleep serves important functions beyond "rest and recuperation," but we don't fully know what these are. The older we are, the less sleep we require. People who sleep less than 4 or greater than 10 hours per night are statistically more likely to have a diminished life expectancy. There is a strong biological tendency among people in general to fall asleep in mid-afternoon. This occurs even after a good night's sleep, and regardless of whether the person has had lunch.

There are five *stages of sleep:* 1: fast waves, *light sleep;* 2: also fast waves and *light sleep* (but not *as* fast and light), occupying 45% of the sleep time of adults; 3: deep sleep with slow (delta) waves; 4: deeper sleep with slower delta waves, occupying 10% of the sleep of adults; 5: *REM (rapid eye movement) sleep,* which occurs every 90–110 minutes; lasts between several minutes (initially) and 20–40 minutes (at the end of the night). REM sleep never starts normal sleep (only patients with narcolepsy start sleep with REM); occurs in human newborns, congenitally blind people, and animals reared in the dark; is associated with increased heart rate, increased blood pressure, decreased tone in the body's skeletal muscles (exception: eye muscles), hyperventilation (excessively deep and rapid breathing), clitoral and penile erection, and vivid, recallable *dreams. Nightmares,* which are usually vivid, recallable dreams, occur in REM sleep. *Night terrors,* which are associated with minimally- or not-remembered, unformed images, occur in stage 4 sleep. A variety of drugs (including barbiturates, alcohol, phenothiazines, benzodiazepines, meprobamate, monoamine oxidase inhibitors, and tricyclic antidepressants) and endogenous depression all decrease REM sleep. When the above-mentioned *drugs* (with the exception of benzodiazepines) are withdrawn, there is *"REM rebound"* in which REM sleep begins earlier in the sleep cycle and lasts longer. Benzodiazepines suppress REM sleep but they do not cause REM rebound.

Endogenously depressed patients have a shortened latent period between sleep onset and REM onset, more frequent eye movement during REM sleep, and less slow-wave sleep. They have more REM sleep early in the night than towards morning, a reversal of the normal REM sleep pattern.

During sleep, patients with peptic ulcers have an increase in un-neutralized acid secretion. In patients with angina pectoris (chest pains due to insufficient blood supply to heart muscle), chest pains are common during sleep. *Intense moods* often impede one's ability to sleep, as can amphetamines, cocaine, caffeine-containing substances, monoamine oxidase inhibitors (MAOIs) and some tricyclic antidepressants such as imipramine.

There are several primary disorders of sleep: In *narcolepsy,* there is excessive daytime sleepiness, *sleep attacks* (consisting of episodes of REM sleep), *cataplexy* (transient muscle weakness, causing falling, initiated by strong emotions), and *hypnagogic hallucinations* (hallucinations occurring upon falling asleep; uniquely, narcoleptics start sleep with REM sleep).

In *pavor nocturnus (night terrors),* the child awakens screaming and is inconsolable, and then returns to sleep after several minutes. If awakened immediately afterwards, he will not remember any fully-formed dream, because night terrors occur during *stage 4 sleep.* Treatment may include bedtime benzodiazepines, which are stage 4 sleep suppressors.

Sleep-walking (somnambulism) also occurs during *stage 4.* The sleep-walk lasts several minutes, is associated with visual agnosia (non-recognition of common objects, e.g., a door), and (like night terrors) is not remembered upon awakening in the morning. The sleep-walk can be dangerous, as the patient can injure himself if he falls.

Enuresis (bedwetting) is very common, occurring in about one-fifth of children over three and under fifteen. It has multiple causes, and often (but not always) occurs in stage 4 of sleep. Successful treatments, depending on the cause, include behavior modification or bedtime imipramine.

People *deprived of sleep* for over 100 hours may develop disorientation, hallucinations and illusions. After 200 hours, ptosis (drooping of the eyelids), nystagmus (jerky movements of the eyes) and tremor can occur. Treatment is for the patient to sleep.

The *sleep apnea* syndrome can be caused by structural collapse of the upper airway or by insufficient brainstem responsiveness to buildup of carbon dioxide. In very young children, the latter can cause *sudden infant death syndrome (SIDS)*. In adults the sleep apnea syndrome is associated with obesity, snoring, apnea (stoppage of breathing), cardiac arrhythmias, hypertension and morning headache. In cases with structural airway collapse, tracheostomy (surgically-created airway from the trachea through the skin of the anterior neck) is commonly used. When there is inadequate brainstem responsiveness to carbon dioxide, the drug theophylline, which among other things stimulates the respiratory center in the brainstem, can be very helpful. Children at severe risk for SIDS often need to sleep with a warning buzzer which immediately notifies the parent or hospital staff that the child has stopped breathing.

In *sleep-related periodic myoclonus,* the patient experiences multiple episodes of motor jerking during the night, and the EEG at these times reveals *K complexes*. The patient has slept poorly, and awakens tired. One treatment is the medication diazepam, which is also an anxiolytic (anti-anxiety) drug.

One final definition: *hypnopompic hallucinations* are hallucinations which occur while the individual is awakening. They have no known major clinical significance.

Sexual Response Cycle

1: Excitement ⎫ ↑ BP, Vent., HR
2: Plateau ⎬ ⎫
3: Orgasm →▷ (Refractory Period in ♂?)
4: Resolution

Chapter 12:

SEX

During the past two decades there has been some decline in the *sexual double standard,* but it still exists to some extent. Also during the past two decades, there has been effective lobbying for women's rights and gay rights. However, public and legal support for almost unlimited sexual freedoms among consenting adults has diminished because of the epidemics of herpes simplex genitalis and acquired immune deficiency syndrome (AIDS).

Endocrinologically, there is no specific sex center in the brain. The male sex hormone pattern is *tonic* (continuous), and the female pattern is *cyclic. Androgen* increases libido in both sexes. During and surrounding *menstruation,* women are more prone to calling in sick at work, being violent, being admitted to psychiatric inpatient units, and experiencing mood changes.

There are four phases to the *sexual response cycle:* ① excitement, where clitoral and penile erection and vaginal lubrication with vascular engorgement can occur within seconds of visual, tactile, auditory or other stimulation. During this and the ② *plateau* and ③ *orgasm* phases which follow, there is increased blood pressure and pulse with hyperventilation and vascular engorgement. During orgasm there are involuntary sphincter contractions, a feeling of climax, and intense pleasure. There is no significant association between the size of a man's flaccid or erect penis and the pleasure he experiences in intercourse. The frequency of orgasms is reportedly greatest for men when they are in their

68

teens and for women in their thirties. Following an orgasm, men experience a *refractory period* during which orgasm is not possible, whereas women can have multiple orgasms. After orgasm is a (4) *resolution* period during which all parameters return to normal. *Masturbation* is extremely common. Virtually all teenage boys, and the majority of teenage girls, do it. Concerning sex and menstruation, it is medically safe to engage in sex during the menses, and during this time pregnancy is far less likely.

Regarding *homosexuality,* most studies since the 1940s have revealed it to be more frequent than what was believed before the 1940s. It is approximately as common in men as in women. About a third of women have gay erotic responses and slightly less than half of men have had a gay experience to orgasm at some time.

A variety of *sexual problems* deserve some attention: Many *drugs* can cause erectile, ejaculatory or orgasmic disturbances. These include neuroleptics, antihypertensives, benzodiazepines, disulfiram, chronic opioid or alcohol abuse, and severe alcohol intoxication. *Medical conditions* associated with sexual dysfunction include Leriche syndrome (occlusion of the lumen of the aorta at its bifurcation, with multiple possible causes), psychomotor epilepsy, Briquet's syndrome, Peyronie's disease (angulation of the shaft of the penis due to connective tissue scarring, cause unknown), diabetes, and endogenous depression. Patients with complete spinal cord transections can have reflex erections with tactile stimulation. Many patients with acute medical illnesses lose interest in sex during the illness. Some manic patients are hypersexual during the manic episode, and many sociopaths are promiscuous. Some people develop sexual dysfunction because they *fear the medical consequences* (e.g., herpes infections, AIDS, myocardial infarction, unwanted pregnancy or injury to a fetus). Practical strategies could dispel some anxiety; e.g., common sense suggests that "heart patients" be supine (lying on back) when first resuming intercourse, which usually can occur when the patient can climb stairs, resume work, or walk a treadmill at 4 MPH. One of the commonest causes of sexual dysfunction is *performance anxiety.*

Concerning more complex sexual dysfunctions, sex therapists often instruct a couple with a sexual problem to engage at home in pleasurable stroking of nongenital (in the first "sessions" at home) and then genital (in subsequent sessions) areas of the body. Specific directions are given not to attempt intercourse in initial sessions. In addition to these *sensate focus exercises,* specialized techniques are used for certain dysfunctions. In the treatment of *premature ejaculation,* the woman is instructed about home exercises in which she will begin masturbating the man, and then will gently squeeze his penis in a prescribed way *(squeeze technique)* before ejaculation is inevitable. In this way, he learns to develop ejaculatory control. An alternative to squeezing the penis is simply stopping the intercourse before ejaculation is inevitable *(stop-start technique)*. *Vaginismus,* which is involuntary contraction of a woman's paravaginal muscles whenever penile penetration is tried, is treated by desensitizing the woman to having something inserted in her vagina by progressively broader insertions of dilators or of her fingers. Occasionally, vaginismus is first identified or confirmed during an examination with a vaginal speculum (a metal instrument resembling two shoe horns attached back-to-back at one end which—after a lubricant is applied—is used to view the uterine cervix and the vaginal walls).

Moving from sex to gender, *gender identity* is the sex one thinks one is. *Transsexual* males (e.g., Christine Jorgenson, Renee Richards) think and feel like women, even before treatment. Transsexualism is a rare gender identity (see p. 45) disturbance with no proven genetic component. It is more common (4:1) in men. Before transsexual surgery is performed, male transsexuals' *sex object choice* (who "turns one on") is males in 75% of cases, and females in 25%. Almost all female transsexuals are attracted to females. Patients requesting transsexual surgery should be evaluated for other disorders and, if these are absent, then (if the desire persists) live as the opposite gender (e.g., men dress as women and take estrogens), and if the latter is acceptably gratifying, have transsexual surgery.

People with *paraphilias* (Most are men.) have sex acts with, or intense recurring fantasies about, non-human or unwilling partners. Examples include *pedophilia* (sex object is a prepubescent child) and *exhibitionism* (exposing genitals to an unsuspecting stranger). Paraphilias rarely cause the patient personal distress; patients are usually referred by legal authorities. Some paraphiliacs commit hundreds of deviant acts. Professional care requires exclusion of coarse brain disease or psychosis as a cause, and includes some combination of psychotherapy, conditioning, or the anti-androgen *medroxyprogesterone.*

Chapter 13.

PSYCHOPATHOLOGY

I. EPIDEMIOLOGY OF MENTAL ILLNESS

According to Dr. Myrna Weissman, at any time about 15% of Americans have diagnosable psychiatric illness. There are some demographic correlates of mental illness:

A. *Socioeconomic status:* Poor people are more prone to psychosis, coarse (organic) brain disease, alcoholism and drug dependence. Male schizophrenics tend to be of lower socioeconomic status than their fathers.

B. *Age:* The risk of mental illness increases with age, with the elderly at greatest risk. Depression and organic mental disorders are the most common illnesses of the elderly. Despite the above, mental health support systems for the elderly are proportionately less than for younger people.

C. *Gender:* Women are more apt to be given psychiatric diagnoses and to receive treatment for mental illness. Diagnoses more common in women are Briquet's syndrome, anorexia nervosa, bipolar disorder, and anxiety disorders. Alcoholism, sociopathy, schizophrenia, mental retardation, and coarse brain diseases in general, are more common in men. Boys are more apt than girls to manifest mental retardation, prematurity, autism, and hyperactivity/MBD syndrome.

D. *Marital status:* Single, divorced, separated and widowed people are at greater risk for most mental illnesses than are married people.

E. *Geography:* Schizophrenia, alcoholism, drug abuse and mental retardation are more common in cities, and coarse brain disease is more common in rural areas.

II. DEFINITIONS

Neurosis is a psychoanalytic concept which means a condition with symptoms such as spontaneous panic attacks, or fears of social situations (e.g., going out of doors or going to school), and which is caused by an unconscious conflict. *Psychosis* (an imprecise word) is defined as a condition which grossly impairs a person's capacity to cope with the ordinary demands of life, usually resulting from hallucinations, delusions or severe cognitive dysfunction. One type of delusion is an *idea of reference,* in which a person believes that events in the environment (e.g., what is said on T.V.) relate ("refer") specifically to him.

Reality perception is the ability to perceive sensations (e.g., to smell, hear, see) accurately. Illusions and hallucinations are the two kinds of impaired reality perception. *Reality testing* is the ability to tell which perceptions are real. A person who hallucinates, but knows the voices he "hears" do not arise from real stimuli, has poor reality perception but good reality testing. Neither hallucinations, illusions, delusions, ideas of reference nor impaired reality perception is pathognomonic of schizophrenia or any other mental illness. A *pathognomonic* symptom or sign is one which, if present, is sufficient for you to make a definite diagnosis. In psychiatry, there are no pathognomonic signs, and they are rare in medicine in general.

III. SPECIFIC SYNDROMES

A. *Bipolar disorder* is a syndrome which is defined by the history of one or more manic or hypomanic (mildly manic) episodes, *regardless* of whether the patient was ever depressed, in the absence of organic brain disease or use of psychostimulant drugs. Our department's criteria (those of Drs. Michael Alan Taylor and Richard Abrams) for a manic episode require rapid or pressured speech; an irritable, expansive, or euphoric mood; and stimulus-bound hyperactivity. Two psychoanalytic explanations of the manic state include ① suspension of superego func-

Genetic Component

tioning and 2) overcompensation for feelings of inferiority. Many patients with bipolar disorder also experience episodes of endogenous depression (see below). When patients experience endogenous depressions alone, the term *unipolar depressive illness* is sometimes used. Interestingly, there is an increased frequency of bipolar disorder among successful creative writers and their *first degree relatives* (relatives with whom a person shares 50% of his genes).

B. Our department's criteria for endogenous depression *(major depressive episode with melancholia)* are 1. a sustained sad, anxious or dysphoric (restless) mood; 2. at least three of the following: (a) appetite loss with weight loss of 5 or more pounds in the preceding 3 weeks; (b) early morning waking; (c) suicidal ideation or behavior; (d) agitation (increased frequency of purposeless motor movements, such as pacing or finger-tapping, in response to a mood) or psychomotor retardation; (e) severe feelings of hopelessness, worthlessness or guilt; (f) diurnal (daily) mood variation where the mood is routinely worse in the morning and gets slightly better as the day progresses; 3. no coarse brain disease; 4. no recent use of reserpine (a drug for high blood pressure) or steroids. *i.e. Reversal of pattern*

Alphamethyldopa (another drug for high blood pressure) and many other medications can also mimic endogenous depression. There is REM sleep loss. There are a number of causal hypotheses, correlates and models for endogenous depression: Based on adoption and twin studies, there is strong suggestive evidence for a genetic causal component in many cases. In one family of Old Order Amish in Pennsylvania (see p. 79), bipolar disorder was associated with autosomal dominant transmission of a single gene on the short arm of chromosome 11. The animal model of depression is that of *learned helplessness*, in which an experimental animal is given electrical shocks (or other aversive stimuli) and not allowed to escape. The animal becomes listless, slow, and withdrawn, doesn't eat, and often dies. McKinney reversed this process in monkeys by giving electroconvulsive therapy. Another hypothesis holds that for unknown (possibly genetic) reasons, there is insufficient norepinephrine at brain receptor sites. Also, one recent study found antibody titers for Borna virus (a "slowly acting" virus never before found in humans) in about 10% of patients with mania or melancholia, and no such titers in controls. Finally, two psychoanalytic theories of depression include 1) guilt over unconscious anger at an ambivalently-loved (see p. 39) person who was lost by death, by separation, or in fantasy; and 2 loss of self-esteem associated with not living up to one's (often-idealized) standards.

C. Our department's criteria for *schizophrenia* are: no abnormalities of consciousness or alertness; the presence of at least one of the following three: 1 emotional blunting; 2 formal thinking disorder 3 one or more first rank signs of Schneider; no coarse brain disease or history of use of hallucinogenic substances. *Emotional blunting* is the inability to experience or convey feelings, manifested by a combination of diminished mood variability, modulation and warmth; an expressionless face and monotonous voice; an inability to elaborate on answers; and an attitude of not caring about friends, family and the future. It is a serious multidimensional sign which must be distinguished from single findings such as the mask-like face or sedation which are often seen as medication side effects. Emotional blunting is sometimes seen in patients with disease of the convexities of the frontal lobes.

A *formal thinking disorder* is the inability to speak relevantly and clearly, using speech patterns such as *nonsequiturs* (eg., Q: "Do you have any brothers or sisters?" A: "I'm a lawyer and a Ph.D."), *neologisms* (newly coined words, e.g., "trentle"), or *drivelling* (glib doubletalk, e.g., "They can't get you at the station, but don't tell the other guys about the booth under the ward"). Many formal thinking disorders are similar to the aphasic speech of some patients with coarse disease of the dominant temporal lobe.

First rank signs (a term coined by Dr. Kurt Schneider) are common in several disorders including (but not exclusive to) schizophrenia. There are five first rank signs: 1. *complete auditory hallucinations,* which are clearly-audible voices perceived as coming from outside one's head and speaking in full sentences; 2. *thought broadcasting,* which is the vivid perception that one's thoughts are literally being transmitted to others by some device such as a loudspeaker within one's head; 3. *delusional perceptions,* which consist of a correct perception (e.g., "Three cars just passed by me . . .") followed illogically by a delusional conclusion (e.g., . . . so I must be in line to become king."); 4. *experiences of influence,* which are experiences that one's thoughts or actions are being controlled by an external force or person (e.g., "The voices outside me made me stab myself"); and 5. *experiences of alienation,* which are perceptions that something has taken

Genetic predisposition
Dopaminergic hyperactivity

over one's thoughts or actions (e.g., "The people inside me are doing my thinking for me.")

For schizophrenia, some causal hypotheses and correlates include the following: Some adoption studies, monozygotic-dizygotic twin comparisons, and chromosome analyses suggest a genetic causal component (see p. 80). (Schizophrenia's *"heritability"* is the extent to which its manifestations result from its genotype). Another theory is that the parents of future schizophrenic children transmit more *"double-bind" messages*. In a double bind message, a person is asked to perform two actions, A and B, which are equal and opposite. If he does A, he cannot do B, and he receives an aversive consequence for doing A. If he does B, he cannot do A, and he receives an aversive consequence for B. Further, he cannot leave the situation or complain that it's insane or impossible. For example, a father tells his son "Go upstairs to your room and try on this blue shirt and this green shirt." The child tries on the blue one and the father says "You didn't like the green shirt." Yet another hypothesis is that schizophrenia is caused by *dopaminergic hyperactivity*.

D. *Focal Coarse (Organic) Brain Disease*

1. In *frontal lobe disease,* there could be abnormalities of concentration, orientation, language, abstraction, judgment, planning, problem-solving ability, and motor regulation; significant personality change is possible. The frontal lobes are discussed at length on p. 90.

2. In *Huntington's chorea,* frontal lobe signs are common. Choreoathetoid (jerky & writhing) body movements reflect atrophy (shrinkage and wasting) of the brain's caudate nucleus, the latter being a highly specific finding on computerized tomographic brain scanning. This gradually progressive, incurable, fatal condition often presents clinically with psychosis, dementia or depression, and the suicide risk is increased. Behavioral changes may occur years in advance of the movement disorder. Huntington's chorea results from autosomal dominant transmission of a genetic defect on chromosome 4. Laboratory testing of blood samples of individuals at risk for the disorder can identify the condition before symptoms and signs appear, but for a variety of reasons some individuals prefer not knowing whether they are afflicted.

3. In *temporal lobe psychomotor epilepsy,* we may find staring and other automatisms; olfactory, gustatory, abdominal, complex visual or auditory hallucinations; déjà vu, hypergraphia (exces-

sive writing, as in multiple daily letters or an overly detailed diary), religiosity, viscosity (talking on the same subject despite strenuous efforts of the interviewer to change subjects), and other manifestations.

4. In some patients with bilateral temporal lobe destruction, there is a combination of placidity, inappropriate orality (e.g., putting inedible objects in the mouth), inappropriate sexuality (e.g., public masturbation) and dementia. This combination is the *Kluver-Bucy syndrome.*

5. In *Wernicke's encephalopathy,* there is a combination of diffuse intellectual dysfunction and either nystagmus or extraocular muscle paralysis, typically of the external rectus muscle innervated by the sixth cranial (abducens) nerve. It results from a combination of a genetic factor and a profound thiamine deficiency, the latter being most frequently associated with alcoholism. Among other brain structures, the periaqueductal gray matter is affected.

6. *Korsakoff's syndrome* is characterized by diffuse intellectual dysfunction with severe memory deficits and consequent *confabulation* (the patient makes up answers when he doesn't know the answer.) Alcoholism is the cause. Among other brain structures the mammillary bodies and fornix are affected. Wernicke's encephalopathy and Korsakoff's syndrome frequently occur together.

7. Patients with *hippocampal* lesions have difficulty with consolidated memory (remembering things from 30 seconds to 30 minutes) and their ability to learn.

E. The criteria of Drs. John Feighner and Eli Robins and associates for *sociopathy* (*antisocial personality disorder*) are one or more findings in five or more of the following nine groups, with onset of at least one before age 15: (1) running away from home and staying out overnight; (2) truancy, suspension, expulsion from school or criticism by teachers for fighting; (3) spouse abuse, infidelity, frequent separations, or at least two divorces; (4) vagrancy or wanderlust; (5) frequent lying or use of an alias; (6) being fired from a job, quitting without another job lined up, or frequent unemployment not explained by seasonal changes; (7) two or more adult fights or use of a weapon; (8) frequent arrests or one or more felony convictions; (9) pimping, prostitution, two or more episodes of venereal disease, or sexual perversion.

The patient is said to have a deficit in conscience [Super Ego] and the capacity to experience guilt, and sometimes the patient and parents are said to have a "lacunar (full of holes, like swiss cheese) superego" which is the product of the parent obtaining vicarious satisfaction from the child's antisocial behaviors.

F. The *obsessive-compulsive* disorder can be a very severe disorder characterized by frequent, unwanted, intrusive, non-psychotic thoughts *(obsessions)* which the patient perceives as ridiculous but is unable to "shake" or suppress, and frequent impractical unnecessary behaviors *(compulsions)* which the patient must perform in response to the obsessions. Common ego defense mechanisms in this disorder are doing and undoing, isolation, intellectualization and reaction formation (see pages 37 and 38). There is an increased prevalence of *Tourette's disorder* (characterized by motor and verbal *tics*, e.g., twitches, grunting, and cursing) in the families of obsessive-compulsive patients.

G. *Conversion disorders* are "pseudoneurologic" or "pseudo-pregnancy" phenomena in which the findings do not conform to standard neuroanatomic pathways or physical findings or laboratory tests. For example, there may be *"hysterical blindness"* in which optokinetic nystagmus, visually-evoked electroencephalographic potentials, and retinoscopy are normal, but the patient believes he cannot see. Another example is pseudopregnancy with swelling of the breasts and abdomen and amenorrhea with no actual pregnancy. Psychoanalytically, conversion disorders have been explained as a somatic resolution of an unconscious conflict. An example would be paralysis of an upper extremity to resolve an unconscious conflict of whether or not to strike a parent. Another explanation that has been offered is that it represents *anosognosia* (nonrecognition) for normal somatic functioning. Followup of many cases has shown "structural" disease at the affected site, meaning that many conversion disorders are not conversion disorders at all. Conversion disorders can be seen concurrently with many other psychiatric syndromes, particularly Briquet's syndrome and antisocial personality disorder.

H. Studies of patients with *hypochondriasis* reveal that it has no validity as a distinct, separate disorder, but instead is a symptom: preoccupation with systemic or mental symptomatology. This is particularly common in, but not exclusive to, endogenous depression, panic disorder, and Briquet's syndrome. When hypochondriasis occurs in endogenous depression, the prognosis for recovery is somewhat diminished. Some patients with conversion disorder experience "la belle indifference"—indifference to symptoms; by definition, hypochondriacal patients do not do so.

I. *Briquet's syndrome (somatization disorder)* is characterized by multiple medically-unexplained symptoms beginning before age 30. It is more common in women. When a woman has this disorder, in her family the men are more likely than the general population to have sociopathy. Physicians rarely offer Briquet's syndrome patients a diagnosis, and often dismiss their complaints with comments like "It's due to stress" or "It's in your head." A physician suspecting the diagnosis should ask the patient if she ever had any of the following seven symptoms which caused her to take medication other than aspirin, alter her life pattern, or see a physician, and for which no diagnosis could be documented: shortness of breath, dysmenorrhea (painful menstruation), bloating, lump in the throat, amnesia, vomiting, or painful extremities. (This is easily remembered by using Othmer's mnemonic "Somatization Disorder Besets Ladies And Vexes Physicians.") If two or more of these seven are positive, the patient has a 90% chance of having Briquet's syndrome, and the diagnosis is then confirmed by questioning from the list of 37 symptoms of somatization disorder in the DSMIIIR.

J. Patients with *panic disorder* begin their illness with panic attacks when there is no reason to panic. The panic attacks include a feeling of dread or impending doom, and two or more of the following: faintness or lightheadedness, palpitations (physical awareness of the heartbeat), shortness of breath, chest pain or discomfort, paresthesias (abnormal sensations, usually "pins and needles"), or a choking or smothering sensation. Sometimes, by conditioning, the panic attacks become associated with an event or object that occurred simultaneously, and the patient may then develop a *phobia* for that event or object. In patients with panic disorder, anxiety attacks can be precipitated by *intravenous lactate*, and during attacks the plasma free fatty acids are elevated. A recent survey revealed that 20% of panic disorder patients have made suicide attempts, but the frequency of completed suicide in panic disorder patients is unknown.

K. The DSMIIIR criteria for *anorexia nervosa* are paraphrased as follows: 1. an intense fear of becoming fat, regardless of actual weight; 2. feeling fat even when gaunt; 3. for women, absence of at least three consecutive menstrual cycles that ordinarily would be expected; and 4. refusal to maintain body weight over a minimal normal weight for age. Despite the use of the term anorexia (which means loss of appetite), the appetite is usually good. The patient, usually a teenage girl, may sometimes gorge herself with food *(bulimia)* and then deliberately vomit or use laxatives. It has been proposed by some that 1) bulimia is a separate disorder and 2) bulimia and anorexia nervosa are variants of endogenous depression.

L. *Transsexuals* feel as if they are members of the opposite sex "trapped" in a body with the wrong genitalia, and wish to dress and act like members of the opposite sex. Some seek sex-change surgery, and have this surgery after careful evaluation and a period of observation. To date, no genetic causal component has been documented. *Hermaphroditism* is different; hermaphrodites possess both ovarian and testicular tissue.

IV. GENETICS OF MENTAL ILLNESS

Until recently, twin and adoption studies were the best way of inferring whether psychiatric conditions have a genetic causal component. From such studies, there was strong suggestive (but not absolute) evidence from such studies that mania, endogenous depression, alcoholism, and sociopathy have such a component. Most psychiatric conditions, as well as most illnesses in general, run in families and are more common in monozygotic than in dizygotic twins. But again, these do not prove a genetic cause. The best means of delineating genetic transmission, *DNA recombination techniques,* recently became available. As a result of these techniques, specific genetic abnormalities have been discovered for a growing number of conditions, including Alzheimer's disease (see p. 58), Huntington's chorea (see p. 75), Tay-Sachs disease (see p. 46), Lesch-Nyhan syndrome (see p. 46), Wilson's disease (see p. 53), developmental reading disorder (see p. 52), (in one family of Old Order Amish and one family of Hassidic Jews) bipolar disorder (see p. 73), and (in 7 British and Icelandic families) schizophrenia (see p. 75).

In the Amish family, autosomal dominant transmission was found to be the product of an abnormal gene on chromosome 11. However, in another study of other families with bipolar disorder, no abnormalities were found on chromosome 11. This suggests that bipolar disorder is a heterogeneous syndrome with a variety of causes.

For psychiatry, as well as for medicine in general, most illnesses are viewed as the product of an interplay of genetic, intrauterine and environmental influences. We rarely think of a single, *sufficient* (absolute) cause.

The *Old Order Amish* (OOA) of Pennsylvania provided a

unique opportunity to examine hypotheses of genetic transmission. The OOA are a closed community descended from 30 progenitors who emigrated from Europe in the 18th century. Geographic concentration, large family sizes, well-established paternity, and a willingness to provide detailed geneologies to a research team led by Dr. Janice Egelund, all made the OOA excellent for pedigree studies. Bipolar disorder occurs with the same frequency and manifestations among the OOA as in the general population, but OOA prohibitions against alcohol use eliminated the confounding effect of alcoholism on studies of mood disorder.

Using DNA analyses, Sherrington found a dominant abnormality on chromosome 5 in seven British and Icelandic families with schizophrenic members. One problem here is that not all the behaviorally-abnormal relatives with chromosome 5 abnormalities met criteria for schizophrenia. Some had schizophrenia-like personality disorders, some had schizophrenia-like psychoses, and some were receiving neuroleptics for unspecified disorders. This lack of diagnostic specificity is a problem with many previous genetic studies of schizophrenia.

Another group found no chromosome abnormalities in a northern Swedish pedigree with schizophrenic members. As is the case for bipolar disorder, it is possible that schizophrenia is a heterogeneous syndrome with multiple causes.

(Finally, as we go to press, the Egelund team found two OOA bipolar patients with no chromosome 11 abnormalities, reducing the significance of their original study.)

Chapter 14:

DRUG ABUSE

What is defined as a drug of abuse in part relates to how society views that substance. *Addiction* is tolerance (requiring progressively increasing doses to obtain the same effect) plus significant withdrawal phenomena (e.g., tremor, seizures, delirium). *Nonaddicting* substances include hallucinogens, neuroleptics, tricyclic antidepressants, lithium and anticholinergics. Of these, only hallucinogens are non-therapeutic.

Classic *addicting* substances are prescription sedative-hypnotics (the most addictive being barbiturates), alcohol, benzodiazepines, propylenediols, opiates and opioids. Cocaine and amphetamines produce considerable tolerance and some withdrawal symptoms, but they can be safely withdrawn abruptly. Opiates and opioids have considerable tolerance and withdrawal symptoms. Although opiates and opioids are rarely fatal in withdrawal, medically-supervised withdrawal in the hospital using clonidine (see p. 83) and dolophine (Methadone, a long-acting opioid) is the preferred treatment.

All of the above substances can be detected in hospital laboratories, with the exception of some hallucinogens such as lysergic acid diethylamide (LSD). The latter is undetectable in most labs because it is ingested as micrograms. Blood levels which are frequently measured are lithium (therapeutic blood level in mania is 1–1.5 meq./L), alcohol (legal limits of drunkenness range from 100–150 meq./L), carbamazepine (therapeutic range 5–12 nanograms/ml.), and tricyclic antidepressants (therapeutic plasma level of imipramine is 150–225 nanograms/ml.).

The *effects of a drug* are influenced by route of administration, the patient's characterologic tendencies, societal norms, and influences from the peer group. *Intoxications* are as follows: *Sedative-hypnotics* and *alcohol* give "drunkenness" with REM sleep suppression, ataxic (staggering, unbalanced) gait, nystagmus, slurred speech, diminished inhibitions and proneness to violence. *Opiate intoxication* produces pinpoint pupils, "nodding" drowsiness, nausea, and euphoria. The histories of opiate addicts often include premature and violent death, suicide and infections. Infections include bacterial endocarditis (infection of the heart valves), abscesses, thrombophlebitis (inflamed veins), tetanus, AIDS, hepatitis and (in countries where it is endemic) malaria (a mosquito-borne protozoan infection).

Anticholinergic toxicity is summarized by the phrase "dry as a bone, red as a beet, mad as a hatter, and blind as a bat." In *cocaine toxicity,* there is increase in blood pressure and pulse, sleeplessness, pleasant and unpleasant mood changes, and sometimes delusions, hallucinations, geometric hallucinations, and *formications* (tactile hallucinations of bugs crawling on the skin, referred to as "cocaine bugs" or *Magnan's sign*), polyopia (seeing multiple images of the same object), and sleeplessness. The cocaine psychosis, as well as mania and epilepsy, have all been explained on the basis of a *"kindling effect"* starting with small, localized un-summed discharges. Complications of cocaine use include decreased coronary artery blood flow with consequent angina pectoris (chest pain due to inadequate blood and oxygen supply to the heart) and myocardial infarction (heart attack), cardiac rhythm abnormalities, and seizures. Pregnant women using cocaine have an increased risk of spontaneous fetal death and of abruptio placentae (tearing of the placenta from the uterine wall). *Amphetamines* are sympathomimetics similar to cocaine which produce increased pulse and blood pressure, mydriasis (enlarging of the pupils), diminished appetite and sleep, euphoria or depression, suspiciousness (sometimes this "paranoia" reaches the point of violence or delusions), and hallucinations. Repeated use of *anabolic steroids* can cause hallucinations, delusions, mania-like syndromes, and depressed mood.

Glue produces drowsiness, euphoria, slurred speech, rhinitis (nasal inflammation), nausea, ataxia, disinhibition, combativeness, hallucinations and illusions. It is most popular among teenagers, especially Hispanic teenagers.

Substances associated with *violence* include amphetamines, alcohol, prescription sedative-hypnotics and, to a lesser extent, cocaine, glue, anabolic steroids, and hallucinogens. Violence caused by intoxication is rare with opiates and opioids.

Intoxications which can approximate "schizophrenic" or psychotic behaviors include amphetamines and cocaine, hallucinogens, alcohol, glue and L-dopa. Amphetamines, apomorphine, L-dopa and cocaine produce stereotypic behavior in animals. Marijuana and alcohol diminish a person's ability to perform complex tasks such as driving a car.

Withdrawal states include the following manifestations: Alcohol, sedative-hypnotics and anxiolytics all can produce "shakes," seizures, and delirium tremens. Seizures and delirium tremens can be fatal. Withdrawal from opiates and opioids includes tachycardia, rhinorrhea (runny nose), lacrimation (tearing), piloerection ("gooseflesh"), joint pain, abdominal pain, nausea and vomiting, leukocytosis (increased white blood cell count) and (rarely) ejaculation. Opiate withdrawal symptoms and signs can be diminished by the antihypertensive (blood-pressure-lowering) agent *clonidine,* an *agonist* (enhancer) of alpha adrenergic receptors. Alpha adrenergic receptors reduce brain and peripheral norepinephrine neuron firing and reduce the quantity of norepinephrine secreted. Discontinuing amphetamines or cocaine can lead to increased appetite, depression and hypersomnia.

Concerning *prevalence,* 2–5% of the American population is alcoholic, and slightly less than 0.3% are addicted to opiates. It is estimated that 30 million Americans have used cocaine and that 5 million use it regularly. Nowadays, abuse of multiple drugs (including alcohol) is becoming more common and single drug-of-choice addictions are becoming less common.

Chapter 15:

SUICIDE AND HOMICIDE

Violence (accidents, suicide and homicide) is the leading cause of death under age 40.

I. SUICIDE

Clinically, it is important to ask any patient with significant behavioral problems if he's contemplating suicide. Suicide is the tenth leading cause of death in the U.S.A., causing almost 30,000 deaths annually, and it is often not reported by medical examiners and coroners, so a "truer" figure of annual suicide mortality may be two or three times this figure. Ninety-five percent of patients who commit suicide have diagnosable psychiatric illness and often visit doctors shortly before they kill themselves. Thus, it follows that suicide is *often preventable.* In fact, it is the second most preventable cause of death in the U.S.A., second only to lung cancer. Sixty-six percent of suicide victims visited their family doctor in the month before their death, and 40% did so in the prior week.

Although suicide is the third leading cause of death in adolescence, the risk of suicide *increases with age,* peaking in middle age for women and over 65 for men. As a rule, the larger the proportion of teenagers in our population, the higher is the teenage suicide rate. In contrast, the larger the proportion of elderly in our population, the lower is the suicide rate among the aged.

Women are more likely to make suicide *attempts,* and *men* are more apt to kill themselves. Native Americans (American Indians) are more apt to kill themselves than are American whites, who are more apt to kill themselves than American blacks. The black-white difference is primarily with the middle-aged and elderly, since young adult blacks are more likely to kill themselves than are young adult whites. High suicide rates occur in Sweden, Austria, Hungary, and Japan, and there are low rates in Ireland and Spain. In general (Austria and Hungary are two exceptions), Catholic countries have low suicide rates. Protestants are more apt to commit suicide than are Catholics.

The *single, widowed, separated and divorced* are more prone to suicide than are married people. Overall, in the U.S., the highest suicide rates are in *urban areas* where large numbers of single people live, although the Western mountain states have the highest suicide rates of any geographic region. Suicide rates fluctuate with *economic cycles,* the highest rates in the U.S. having been during the Great Depression.

Psychiatric diagnoses most closely associated with suicide are endogenous depressions (lifetime suicide risk in bipolar disorder is 15%), non-endogenous depressions, alcoholism, schizophrenia and serious medical/systemic illnesses. The suicide rate of dialysis patients exceeds the national average, and rates are higher for patients with rheumatoid arthritis, peptic ulcer, cancer, chronic obstructive pulmonary disease, and tic douloureux (severe facial pain due to compression or inflammation of the trigeminal nerve). The majority of patients who commit suicide are not psychotic.

Intelligence does not ward off suicide. Sixty percent of people who kill themselves have made *previous suicide attempts,* and 10% of people who make suicide attempts will eventually kill themselves. Suicide is most likely to occur in patients *recently discharged* from the hospital. Suicide rates are usually highest in the *Spring.* The presence of *suicide prevention centers* in a city does not greatly diminish the city's suicide rate, although individual patients may be helped.

Suicide tends to run in families, and one adoption study suggested genetic transmission. However, in that study it was hard to determine whether it was depression, suicidality, or both, that was transmitted.

High rates are seen among police, dentists, musicians, lawyers, and female physicians. The majority of patients who kill themselves *talk about suicide,* either spontaneously or if questioned. Decisions about hospitalizing a suicidal patient often will include the extent of family supports at home.

One study revealed comparatively lower concentrations of 5 hydroxy indoleacetic acid (5-HIAA, a metabolite of the indoleamine serotonin) in the cerebrospinal fluid of people who committed suicide by violent means (e.g., firearms, hanging, or jumping from high places). The significance of this is uncertain, but may reflect diminished serotonin metabolism in one subgroup of depressed patients.

II. HOMICIDE

This is the eleventh leading cause of death in this country, and the rate has recently increased to its highest level ever. It was also high during the Great Depression.

Perpetrators (those committing the homicide) and victims are more likely to be teenagers and young adults, with the *peak age range* between *15 and 34.* Homicide is the second leading cause of death in adolescence. Perpetrators and victims are more likely to be *men.* Relatively more homicide victims are related to their killers by marriage (e.g., spouses, stepchildren, step-parents) than by blood. Homicide is primarily *intra-racial,* with whites killing whites, blacks blacks, Chicanos Chicanos, etc. The highest homicide rates in the U.S. are for blacks. Regarding *religion,* perpetration by Catholics is more common than by Protestants. But socioeconomic status plays a much greater role in explaining ethnic differences in homicide rates than an intrinsic tendency toward violence. Homicide is more common among the *poor,* and in urban ghettos. Unfortunately, homicide statistics do not control for variables such as diagnosis of sociopathy, being reared in a one-parent household, or experiencing coma from accidents such as falls from unscreened apartment house windows.

Past violence often predicts future violence. At least half of people who commit violent crimes are intoxicated with some substance, but this does not prove that the intoxicant was the cause; it may have been disinhibition in a person who intended violence before the violent act. *Diagnoses* associated with violence include sociopathy, alcoholism, drug dependence, Briquet's syndrome, psychomotor epilepsy, and mania. For women, violent behavior is more common close to or during menstruation.

[Handwritten annotations:]

- Territoriality
- Dominance Hierarchies
- Pair Bonding
-
- Contact Comfort
- Fixed Ax pattern → Instinctive Behavior
  - Innate Releaser
-

Chapter 16:
- Imprinting
ETHOLOGY
- Reservoir of Energy
- Displacement
- Animal's Umwelt

— Aggression
⇒ Med Hpotha → Rage
— Late " → Predator Aggression

Ethology is the study of animal behavior. Certain principles of behavior (e.g., conditioning) can be learned from non-human animals and then extrapolated to, or tested on, humans. Invasive experiments on the causes and treatment of behavioral and other medical disorders can be performed on non-human animals and then tested on humans.

Some important ethologic concepts are as follows: *Territoriality* means that an animal, two mates and their offspring, or some larger social unit, identifies a location as its own, can find it from a distance, and will usually defend it against other species or members of the same species. *Dominance hierarchies* are systems of ranking animals within a group. This occurs in many social species. *Pair bonding* refers to continuous pairing with a mate for the purpose of reproduction. Variations of this include *annual monogamy* (bonding with one mate each year), *polygamy*, and *polyandry* (one female mates with multiple males). *Promiscuity* is non-continuous pairing with many mates.

Dr. Harry Harlow studied the effects of *deprivation of attention and affection* on monkeys. He found that upon being returned to live with other monkeys, these deprived monkeys manifested decreased playfulness and increased fearfulness and aggressivity. They rejected sex when given ample opportunity for it, and manifested rocking movements. This could be reversed when they were placed continuously with "peer monkeys." Some of these abnormal behaviors could be prevented by placing the isolated monkeys with a cloth "mother surrogate," which provided *contact comfort*.

Regarding instinctive and learned behavior, a *fixed action pattern* is an instinctive behavior that requires a specific stimulus called an *innate releaser* to trigger it. To be called a fixed action pattern, a behavior must occur 1) the same way each time the stimulus is presented; 2) the first time the releaser is presented, before any learning can take place; 3) in all members of the species 4) and in individuals reared in isolation from members of the species.

Imprinting means that there are certain periods in an animal's development (e.g., immediately after hatching in Dr. D. M. Spaulding's chicks) where what is learned (e.g., to respond to Spaulding as a parent) is learned indelibly, as if "stamped" (imprinted) on the animal's brain.

Dr. Konrad Lorenz described a "reservoir" of energy (*action specific energy*) associated with instinctive behavior. If an instinctive response is continually evoked by the right stimuli, this reservoir will be temporarily depleted. The instinctive response will reappear only with buildup of new energy stores.

Dr. Niko Tinbergen discovered that when an animal has a conflict between two instinctive behaviors, it will manifest an impractical, third behavior. For example, if a chicken is confronted by an enemy it would like to attack, but the enemy is much larger and heavier, the chicken may begin pecking at imaginary food. This is called *displacement* and has been used as a model of human neurosis.

Dr. Jacob von Uexkull is responsible for the idea that, of a large number of stimuli, an animal responds primarily to those which are pertinent to its survival. This tendency to respond to these critical stimuli is called that animal's *umwelt*.

Different types of aggression have been identified in animals, and have been linked to functioning of specific brain areas. For example, when the medial hypothalamus of a cat is electrically stimulated, the cat manifests *rageful aggression*, with snarling and hissing. When the cat's lateral hypothalamus is stimulated, quiet stalking and biting directed at natural prey (*predatory aggression*) occurs.

Aggression occurs in all species, but man is the only species that commits suicide. Of course, animals take serious risks (e.g., birds that chirp warnings), and some don't care well for themselves (e.g., monkeys experiencing experimental learned helplessness), but this is not suicide.

Chapter 17:

NEUROPSYCHOLOGY AND BEHAVIORAL NEUROLOGY: DISCIPLINES THAT ADDRESS COGNITIVE FUNCTIONS SUCH AS MEMORY

Neuropsychology is the basic science linking areas of the brain with specific behaviors. *Behavioral neurology* is the clinical subspecialty on the interface of psychiatry and neurology which links dysfunction of specific areas of the brain with abnormal behaviors. Behavioral neurology usually deals with dysfunctions of the secondary and tertiary cortices of the brain.

Primary cortex, such as the visual cortex in Brodmann's area 17 of the occipital lobe, receives uninterpreted stimuli such as light or sound. *Secondary cortex*, occupying areas such as Brodmann's areas 18 and 19 (which surround area 17), organizes incoming sensations into recognizable patterns (such as the image of a flower) that even a preverbal child might find familiar. In *tertiary cortex*, which comprises areas such as the angular gyrus of the parietal lobe, sensory patterns are interpreted, linked to other cortical regions, and acted upon. For example, the statement "What a sweet-smelling rose!" reflects the linkage of smell and sight, the identification and explanation of what is perceived, and the communication of the idea to someone else. Secondary and tertiary cortical functions are sometimes loosely referred to as *cognitive functions* (and the behavioral neurologic examination is sometimes called a cognitive examination), even though "cognitive" is literally defined as "knowing," or "becoming acquainted with."

The *dominant hemisphere* refers to the cerebral hemisphere that is organized to express language. In 97% of people (99% of right-handers and 60% of left-handers), the dominant hemisphere is the left. The dominant hemisphere processes information in a sequential, step-by-step fashion; the nondominant hemisphere processes information in a *Gestaltic* (whole pictures at a glance), intuitive fashion.

The *corpus callosum* and other deep cortical structures are responsible for communicating between the two hemispheres. For example, the corpus callosum must be intact for a person to tie his shoelaces with his eyes closed, so that "his right hand knows what his left hand is doing."

The functions of the *frontal lobes* can be remembered by the mnemonic device COLA J.M. (concentration, orientation, language, abstracting ability, judgment and problem solving, and motor regulation). With the exception of language, frontal lobe cognitive functions cannot be localized to the left or the right hemisphere; the frontal lobes act "in concert." *Concentration* is tested by having the patient spell a five letter word (e.g., earth) forwards. If his *spelling* (a dominant parietal lobe function) is intact, then ask him to spell the word backwards. Another test of concentration is to have the patient subtract sevens serially from 100 (100-7 = 93; 93-7 = 86, etc.). *Global orientation* is tested by having the patient tell you the day of the week, the date, the year, and the season, as well as the floor he is on, the building he is in, and the city, state, and county. *Understand but can't speak properly*

Expressive language (the transmission of a thought to the mus-*ie. Artic*cles of articulation) is largely a function of Broca's area (located *Properly* in the posterior inferior region of the dominant frontal lobe). Damage to Broca's area gives *Broca's aphasia*, characterized by slow, labored, dysarthric (mispronounced, such as "Messodist Epistopal" for "Methodist Episcopal") telegraphic (like a telegram, leaving out small words like "to," and "if," e.g., "Don't write, send money.") speech. *Transcortical motor aphasia* results from damage to the frontal lobe deep to Broca's area, in which the patient has a paucity (insufficiency, sparseness) of speech, which is labored. But full (although brief) sentences are used; the speech is not telegraphic.

Abstracting ability is tested by asking the patient about similarities among objects, e.g., "In what way are an airplane and a bicycle similar?" The best response is one in which the objects are categorized, e.g., "They are both forms of transportation," rather than one in which some common characteristic is identified, e.g., "They both have wheels." *Judgment* and *problem-solving ability* are assessed by your "judging" how the patient solves his life's problems (e.g., My judgment was impaired when I awakened from anesthesia following knee surgery and asked the operating room nurses "Is it O.K. if I breathe now?"), or how he manages a hypothetical task such as "If I had two bookshelves and 18 books, and I had to put twice as many books on one shelf as on the other, how many books should I put on each shelf?" By the way, if you can answer this question, you're probably ready for Part I of the Boreds. If you can't, you still may be ready for the Boreds, and you're definitely qualified to hold a high elective office.

Stimulus-resistant motor regulation involves the ability to control one's motor functions based upon reasoning, despite the presence of visual or other stimuli that might lead a person with brain dysfunction to lose control over these actions. For example, you instruct the patient "When I touch my nose, you touch your mouth," and proceed to touch your nose. If the patient responds by touching his nose (You must be sure he understood the question.), he has demonstrated *echopraxia*, an example of *stimulus-bound* motor dysregulation seen in *catatonia*, a condition which can be caused by endogenous depression, mania, frontal lobe coarse brain disease, drug intoxications or side effects, or schizophrenia.

The posterior portion of the superior temporal gyrus of the dominant hemisphere is *Wernicke's area*, where words are linked to visual images or unformed thoughts. Patients with disease of this area have difficulty understanding your speech, and trouble naming objects (e.g., a wristwatch or pen). They manifest drivelling speech, nonsequiturs and neologisms (see p. 74). However, if Broca's area is intact, the words, however irrelevant or unhelpful, are still articulated fluently. One way of distinguishing the speech of a patient with *Wernicke's aphasia* from that of a schizophrenic with a formal thinking disorder is that schizophrenics are usually able to use polysyllabic words, and Wernicke's aphasic patients are usually unable to do so.

The tracts linking Wernicke's area to Broca's area are in the *supramarginal gyrus* and the *arcuate fasciculus*, so that damage to either disconnects Broca's from Wernicke's area and produces *conduction aphasia*. In conduction aphasia, the patient has normal comprehension of speech (so he can correctly point or gesture in response to a request), but his speech is like that of a Wernicke's aphasic patient, and he is dramatically unable to repeat words or sentences spoken to him. He can read for comprehension, but he cannot read aloud correctly.

When there is massive damage to the dominant hemisphere affecting both Broca's and Wernicke's area, the patient shows *global aphasia*, which has features of both Broca's and Wernicke's aphasia: he cannot speak fluently, cannot understand others' speech, and cannot repeat what he hears. Please note that for all aphasic patients, the ability to repeat and the ability to compensate by writing are impaired.

In addition to speech, other language functions are served by the *dominant temporoparietal region*. The patient should be able to *point to named objects* when you ask him to do so, such as when you say "Show me a button." *Letter gnosis* (*gnosis* means "to know") is tested by asking the patient to identify several letters (e.g., MGW) that he is shown. To test *number gnosis*, ask the patient to identify numbers presented to him. *Reading* is tested by asking the patient to read words (e.g., SEVEN) and sentences (e.g., SEE THE BLACK DOG). *Reading comprehension* is tested by asking the patient to perform an action based upon what he has read (e.g., TOUCH YOUR LEFT HAND TO YOUR RIGHT EAR, which is also a test of *right-left orientation*, the latter being a dominant parietal lobe function). To evaluate *writing* skills, ask the patient to "Write a sentence. It can be about anything you want."

The *dominant parietal lobe* has a variety of functions beyond right-left orientation. *Finger gnosis* is the patient's ability to name the finger (e.g., "thumb," "ring finger") at which you point. *Calculation* must be tested beyond what is rotely memorized (e.g., "How much is 7 + 8?"). You should require the patient to "carry" one or two digits (e.g., "How much is 85–27?"). *Gerstmann's syndrome*, which is the co-existence of left-right disorientation, finger agnosia, impaired calculating ability, and impaired writing ability, commonly occurs with disease of the *angular gyrus*, an important tertiary cortical area of the dominant parietal lobe.

Other functions of the dominant parietal lobe include symbolic categorization, graphesthesia, and stereognosis. *Symbolic categorization* is tested by asking the patient to identify consanguineous (blood) relationships in a family (e.g., "What would be the relationship to you of your brother's father?")

Graphesthesia is tested by asking the patient to supinate (palms placed as if they were holding bowls of soup) his hands, close his eyes, and identify letters printed on his palms, one at a time, with an implement (e.g., the cap of a ballpoint pen) that leaves no ink or graphite stains on his hand. The left hand should be tested first, then the right. When the right hand is tested, it indicates functioning of the left (the dominant one 97% of the time) parietal lobe. When the left hand is tested it indicates functioning of the right parietal lobe and the corpus callosum (the latter because naming the letter requires that information cross from the right to the left hemisphere).

Stereognosis is also tested with the patient's eyes closed and hands supinated. You place various objects (e.g., different coins) sequentially in each palm and instruct the patient to "Feel this coin with your fingers and tell me what it is." Again, as above, the left hand (right parietal lobe and corpus callosum) is tested before the right hand (left parietal lobe).

Kinesthetic praxis is tested by asking the patient to mimic your hand and finger positions, after you instruct him "What I do with my right hand, you do with your right hand, and what I do with my left hand, do with your left hand." When the right hand is tested, the left parietal lobe is being evaluated, and vice versa. This is not a test of callosal functioning.

In addition to graphesthesia, stereognosis, and kinesthetic praxis, the *nondominant parietal lobe* has other functions. These include constructional praxis, dressing, east-west orientation, and a group of functions characterized as *recognition of the familiar*. *Constructional praxis* is the ability to copy the outline of a geometric shape (e.g., a triangle) or other object (e.g., a key) on a blank piece of paper without lifting one's pencil from the page. *Dressing dyspraxia* occurs when a patient has pronounced difficulty when asked to remove his shirt and then put it on again. For example, the patient may put his feet through his shirtsleeves. To test for *east-west orientation*, tell the patient: "If behind you is north, point to the direction that would be east." Nondominant parietal lesions can also lead to *prosopagnosia* (nonrecognition of familiar faces, e.g., "That woman looks something like my mother, but she isn't; she's an impostor.") *anosognosia* (nonrecognition of obvious physical signs of disease, e.g., *Anton's syndrome*, which is failure to recognize one's blindness, or *Babinski's agnosia*, the nonrecognition of one's hemiparalysis, the latter leading to risky attempts to arise from one's bed and walk), and *left spatial neglect* (which leads to behaviors such as not shaving the left side of one's face, or routinely bumping into objects on the left).

The nondominant hemisphere in general (the function cannot be localized further) serves the function of active perception. *Active perception* is the ability to mentally rotate the image of an object without tilting one's head. It is tested by showing the patient an "upside-down" or "sideways" picture of an object (e.g., a hat, a baby) and asking him to name it without turning his head. If he cannot name it correctly, you then turn it "right side up." If he then names it correctly, the deficit was in active perception. If he cannot name if after you rotate it upright, the defect was impaired *naming* (*dysnomia*, a dominant temporoparietal function).

Another nondominant hemisphere function is *prosody*, the emotional and melodic component of speech. *Spontaneous prosody* and *gesturing* are assessed simply by listening to the patient speak and watching his gestures. An abnormality in this area is *expressive dysprosodia*: the patient speaks monotonously with minimal gesturing. However, typically he will tell you that he cares more intensely than he looks, and that he just cannot convey these feelings adequately. To test *comprehension of prosody*, ask the patient to identify a mood you are miming, following which you nonverbally convey anger (e.g., by clenching your fists and jaw), happiness, sadness or anxiety. Then you stand behind the patient and speak several emotionally neutral sentences (e.g., "The boy went to the store."), changing the mood with each sentence. Following each sentence, you ask the patient to state whether the sentence was spoken angrily, happily, sadly or anxiously. Interestingly, expressive prosody localizes to the portion of the nondominant frontal lobe that parallels Broca's area in the dominant hemisphere, and comprehension of prosody localizes to the area paralleling Wernicke's area.

The *occipital lobes* are tested by asking the patient to identify a visual pattern in the presence of a distracting background (identifying camouflaged objects).

Memory can be divided into five phases: 1. Sensations immediately received by the *primary cortex* are stored in the *sensory memory store*. If not attended to within seconds, the sensations are forgotten. 2. These sensations are organized into patterns by secondary cortex, and *attention* is paid by frontal lobe activation. 3. If the patient *concentrates*, he can briefly *retain* some information (e.g., a series of three words or eight numbers), in part a frontal lobe function. This retained information is in the *short-term memory store*, tested by stating three unrelated words (e.g., book, house, candle), or a sequence of 4 to 8 numbers, and asking the patient to repeat these immediately after each presentation. This requires frontal lobe functioning, but has not been localized solely to the frontal lobe. 4. If the patient rehearses, the memory becomes *consolidated* within 30 seconds to 30 minutes. This requires functioning of at least one *hippocampus*. 5. In the *long-term store*, information can be remembered beyond 30 minutes, sometimes as long as a lifetime (e.g., the words to a song you learned when you were ten). It is easily testable, and it requires tertiary cortical functioning, but is not localizable. Either spontaneously or by cuing, these long-term memories can be *retrieved*.

When brain function is so compromised that the patient is unable to attend, concentrate and rehearse, then information is not retained from the time of onset of the compromised function to the time the brain functioning is restored. Here, *anterograde amnesia* has occurred. When the patient cannot retrieve information that was well-learned before brain function was compromised, *retrograde amnesia* has occurred.

Chapter 18:

EMOTIONS, MOTIVATION, AND HYPOTHALAMIC FUNCTIONS

Emotions are feelings or aroused mental states with both cognitive and systemic physiologic components. *Motivations* are the goals and drives that lead an individual to take action. Emotions and motivations can be the product of conditioning (e.g., The pleasure of seeing one's manuscript in print is a learned pleasure.) or reflect systemic physiologic functioning (e.g., As a result of excessive perspiration which changes plasma osmolality, one becomes thirsty and looks for a water fountain.). The cerebral cortex addresses the cognitive component, and the hypothalamus monitors and responds to the *internal milieu* (systemic physiologic functioning). Mediating between the cortex (especially the *limbic association cortex* on the medial and inferior surfaces of the cerebral hemispheres in portions of the frontal, parietal and temporal lobes) and the hypothalamus is the *limbic system*. Limbic system structures include the septal area, the substantia innominata, the amygdala, the piriform cortex, and the hippocampus. It has been said, but not proven, that in humans the limbic system "drives the cortex" (e.g., Mr. Jones's thoughts are pessimistic because of an emotion of sadness.).

In experimental animals, stimulation of the *lateral hypothalamus* elicits *anger*, and lateral hypothalamic *lesions* produce *placidity*. The *lateral hypothalamus* contains a *feeding center*, and the medial hypothalamus a *satiety center*. Electrical stimulation of the *lateral hypothalamus* causes dilation (widening) of skin blood vessels and cessation of shivering, leading to *lowered body temperature*. Stimulation of the *posterior hypothalamus conserves* and *generates heat*. The *suprachiasmatic nucleus* influences *circadian* (24-hour) *rhythms* for such functions as corticosteroid release, drinking, feeding, and motor activity.

Anxiety is a commonly-experienced emotion which is sometimes normal (e.g., while driving on a winding mountain road that has no guard rails). In moderate amounts, anxiety can be a motivating influence (e.g., while studying for the Boreds). However, it is inherently uncomfortable. Its cognitive component often consists of a sense of impending doom, failure, or embarrassment. Its systemic physiology is a "fight or flight" response which can result in *tachycardia* (rapid pulse), *palpitations* (see p. 78), increased systolic blood pressure, chest pain, lightheadedness, hyperventilation (see p. 65), paresthesias (see p. 78), tension or vascular headache, muscle aches, trembling, nausea, vomiting, diarrhea, increased urinary frequency, decreased sexual arousal, pallor (paleness) of the skin, *exophthalmos* (protruding eyes) and sweating. Anxiety can increase pain, and pain can increase anxiety.

Anxiety decreases the clotting time in blood donors. Prior to speeches, public speakers show increased blood levels of norepinephrine, triglycerides and free fatty acids. Before income tax deadlines, the serum cholesterol of accountants rises. Prior to examinations, the skin free fatty acid levels of students with acne rises.

Chapter 19:

BEHAVIORAL NEUROCHEMISTRY

Immunocytologic (see p. 100) and genetic recombination techniques bring neurobiology to the brink of striking discoveries about molecular mechanisms of behavior and behavioral disorders. There could be out-and-out cures of some genetically-caused behavioral disorders within the next few decades. For example, if a specific genetic abnormality is discovered, repair of the defective gene by retroviruses, or replacement of a missing enzyme, could be curative.

Now, we have helpful but relatively primitive concepts about the neurochemistry of major behavioral disorders and their treatment. We are limited by a) the probability that most psychiatric disorders as we now know them are not unitary diseases, but instead are *syndromes* (clusters of common signs and symptoms), each with multiple causes (a pattern resembling that of mental retardation); b) the fact that drugs which relieve symptoms of specific psychiatric syndromes have multiple actions (e.g., lithium, which cures manic episodes, inhibits both monoamine release [see p. 101] and phosphoinositide [see p. 101] breakdown.), providing no definitive clue about the syndromes' causes; c) the fact that laboratory correlates of disorders (e.g., the high norepinephrine-to-cortisol ratios in the urine of post-traumatic stress disorder patients) often do not reveal either the sources of the abnormal quantities (or abnormal ratios) of substances studied (e.g., Where was the excess norepinephrine manufactured?) or the underlying pathophysiologic mechanisms (e.g., Why isn't more cortisol released in this "anxiety disorder?"); d) the fact that some data appears contradictory (e.g., lithium, an effective antidepressant for patients with bipolar disorder, depletes catecholamines, contradicting the catecholamine hypothesis of affective disorder, which holds that depression results from insufficient norepinephrine at neuronal receptors).

I. GENERAL NEUROHISTOLOGY AND NEUROPHYSIOLOGY

To begin to understand current and future neurochemical theories of behavior, it is important to be familiar with some well-documented neurochemical data: The *neuron* (nerve cell) is unique among cells because of the extent of its specialization and its interconnection with other cells. Unlike other cells, neurons cease cell-division during fetal development (after some of these interconnections are established). Some neurons' *axons* (extensions of the cell body which relay messages) or *dendrites* (extensions which receive messages) are connected to thousands of other neurons and extend to distant areas of the brain. The adult brain contains about 10^7 neurons.

One crucial property of neurons is that their membranes (outer walls) are excitable and generate electrical currents. This occurs because of the neuronal membrane's capacity to *pump ions* from the cell and then to re-accept them through *ion channels*. For example, at a given time, a membrane is polarized by its extruding two sodium ions (total charge $+2$) for every potassium ion (total charge $+1$) it re-accepts. This leads to a propensity to depolarize, and sodium channels open to re-accept sodium. This causes a wave of electrical activity, called an *action potential*, to be transmitted from the dendrite to the cell body and then to the axon. External control of this process occurs when neurotransmitter substances are released by the axons of adjacent neurons and are bound by receptors on dendritic, cell body, or axonal surfaces.

There are many neurotransmitter substances. These include "classics" (meaning that I learned about them in the 1960s) like dopamine, norepinephrine, serotonin and acetylcholine, which are manufactured in axonal terminals, neuropeptides such as endorphins and cholecystokinin (the latter originally thought to exist only in the gastrointestinal system), which are produced in the cell body, and amino acids such as gamma amino butyric acid (GABA) and L-glutamic acid, which are produced both in the axon and the cell body. During the past decade, many substances were identified as neurotransmitters. In 1988, testosterone and progesterone, sex hormones produced outside the brain, and pregnenolone and dihydroepiandrosterone, sex hormones manufactured inside as well as outside the brain, were identified as neurotransmitters.

II. IMMUNOCYTOLOGIC TECHNIQUES

As elegantly explained by Joseph T. Coyle in the 1988 *American Psychiatric Press Textbook of Psychiatry*, modern immunocytochemical techniques enable us to better understand the connections and chemistry of neurons. Neurotransmitters under study in human or other animal neurons are *antigens* (substances treated by the body as "foreign," stimulating antibody production) when injected into mice. When a given neurotransmitter/ antigen to be studied is injected into mice, the mice manufacture antibodies to the neurotransmitter in the lymphocytes of their spleens. Researchers then attach these antibodies to myeloma cells (cells derived from the plasma cell cancer multiple myeloma), a linkage which causes these new antibodies to reproduce themselves. Then these antibodies are "tagged" by linkage to a second antibody that has been attached to a visible marker such as horseradish peroxidase (I always knew horseradish was valuable besides at mealtimes.). This complex, altered, visualizable antibody to the specific brain neurotransmitter is then injected into brain tissue where antigen-antibody complexes are visualized and mapped, localizing the sites of the cells that produced the original neurotransmitter under study.

III. SPECIFIC NEUROTRANSMITTERS

A. *Catecholamines in General*

The catecholamine neurotransmitters form a single biosynthetic pathway. The amino acid *L-tyrosine* is catalyzed by the enzyme *tyrosine hydroxylase* to *L-DOPA*, which is catalyzed by DOPA decarboxylase to *dopamine*, which is catalyzed by dopamine beta hydroxylase to *norepinephrine*, which is catalyzed by phenylethanolamine N-methyl transferase (under corticosteroid influence) to *epinephrine*. Tyrosine hydroxylase is the *rate-limiting enzyme* in this feedback pathway: When the concentration of catecholamines in the axonal terminal exceeds the terminal's storage capacity, this excess inhibits tyrosine hydroxylase. Although catecholamines comprise one continuous biosynthetic pathway, each has distinct functions and separate areas of particular concentration within the brain.

At the axon terminal, catecholamines are stored in *vesicles* by an active process requiring energy and serving two functions: 1. Vesicles protect catecholamines from breakdown by the intracellular enzyme *monoamine oxidase*. 2. When the action potential reaches the axon terminal, it opens channels for the *influx of calcium*, leading in turn to the fusion of vesicles with the axonal membrane at the synapse, thus releasing the catecholamine by *exocytosis*. Neurons can produce and receive more than one neurotransmitter. Usually, this *co-localization* involves a classic neurotransmitter and a neuropeptide, but two classic neurotransmitters also can coexist.

Once released into the synapse, one of several things can happen to a catecholamine neurotransmitter: 1. It can be degraded by the enzyme *catechol-O-methyl transferase*. 2. It can be taken back into its cell of origin by "reuptake." In both cases, it cannot perform its function of neurotransmission. 3. Neurotransmission occurs only if the neurotransmitter in the synapse is bound to, and incorporated within, a *receptor site* on the axonal, cell body or dendritic membrane of an adjacent neuron. Interestingly, receptors don't respond exclusively to the body's natural (endogenous) neurotransmitters. For example, *neuroleptic drugs* have an affinity for *dopamine receptors*.

Some events at dendritic receptor sites do not involve ion channels. These events include the activation of enzymes which produce intracellular *second messengers*, which activate additional cellular enzymes. Examples of second messengers include *cyclic AMP* and *phosphoinositides*.

B. *Specific Catecholamines*

1. *Dopamine*: Dopamine-containing neurons in the *substantia nigra* project to the caudate nucleus and putamen (which are

components of the "basal ganglia") and to the frontal cortex. Because the main function of the basal ganglia is the smooth execution of muscle movements, it is easy to understand why degeneration of the nigrostriatal dopamine pathway is associated with *Parkinson's disease*, which is manifested by pill-rolling tremor, rigidity, expressionless face, drooling, and shuffling gait. Also, Parkinson's disease sometimes causes depression, or dementia with prominent frontal symptoms. Because of the above, it is also easy to understand why a Parkinson-like syndrome can be induced by neuroleptic drugs, which block dopamine receptors (Fortunately, this pseudo-Parkinsonism is reversible.), and why L-DOPA, a dopamine precursor, is a useful treatment of Parkinson's disease.

In addition, dopaminergic cell bodies in the *arcuate nucleus of the hypothalamus* send axons ending in the pituitary's venous sinuses. This inhibits the release of *prolactin*, a pituitary hormone which causes production of breast milk. This finding has led researchers to use prolactin production as an indirect measure of dopaminergic transmission: The more the prolactin identified in the blood, the less dopaminergic transmission presumably occurred. Neuroleptic drugs, as dopamine blockers, enhance prolactin release. This explains the occasional occurrence of pseudolactation (production of breast milk in a nonpregnant woman) in women taking neuroleptics.

2. *Norepinephrine*: The *locus coeruleus* (Coeruleus means blue and the locus in blue.), which is located bilaterally on the floor of the pons, is the principal nucleus (collection of cell bodies) of noradrenergic (norepinephrine-containing) neurons. In fact, this locus contains over 50% of the noradrenergic neurons in the central nervous system. Axons from locus neurons contact thousands of neurons throughout the cerebral cortex, cerebellum, thalamus, and hypothalamus. *Norepinephrine* has 2 classes of receptors, each with two subtypes: alpha-1, alpha-2, beta-1 and beta-2. Alpha-2 receptors lie on the pre-synaptic noradrenergic cell body. When activated, alpha-2 receptors inhibit firing of noradenergic neurons, decreasing the norepinephrine released, probably by reducing calcium influx. The antihypertensive drug *clonidine* is an *alpha-2 agonist* (meaning that it buttresses alpha-2 action). This explains why clonidine sometimes has an anti-anxiety effect and decreases symptoms of alcohol, narcotic and nicotine withdrawal, and why *yohimbine*, an alpha-2 antagonist, can increase anxiety.

C. *Serotonin, an Indoleamine Neurotransmitter*

The group of *median raphe nuclei* surrounding the midbrain aqueduct contain most of the cell bodies of serotonin-releasing neurons. Serotoninergic neurons connected to the cerebral cortex are associated with REM sleep (see p. 65). Those connected to the limbic system are associated with aggression, and those connected to the spinal cord affect pain sensitivity.

D. *Acetylcholine*

Neuronal cell bodies in the basal forebrain produce cholinergic (pertaining to the neurotransmitter acetylcholine) innervation to the cerebral cortex, hippocampus, and limbic structures. The *nucleus basalis* of *Meynert*, the globus pallidus, and two other brain areas, send axons of cholinergic neurons to the cortex. Acetylcholine has an important function in memory. Delirium occasionally occurs as a side effect of *anticholinergic drugs* such as *atropine*, scopolamine, anti-Parkinson agents, tricyclic antidepressants, and neuroleptics. As we have seen before, the latter two drug categories also act on other neurotransmitters.

E. *GABA and L-Glutamic Acid*

The amino acids *GABA* (gamma amino butyric acid) and *L-glutamic acid* are, respectively, the primary inhibitory and excitatory neurotransmitters in the brain. When GABA is released and received, inhibition occurs at the receptor neuron. This inhibition is believed to result from increases in *chloride ion permeability*. Neurons producing GABA and L-glutamic acid are found throughout the brain. Blockade of GABA receptors with the nontherapeutic drugs bicuculline or picrotoxin causes seizures. Unlike the long noradrenergic and dopaminergic neurons, GABA-ergic neurons are short-range, local-circuitry neurons. Glutamate is the excitatory neurotransmitter of cortical and hippocampal pyramidal cells.

F. *Endorphins*

Endorphins are neuropeptide neurotransmitters that bind to the same receptors as do opioid narcotic analgesic medications. This suggests that they are endogenous (within the body) analgesic substances. One site of their analgesic effects is the dorsal horn of the spinal cord where they inhibit the activity of pain-conveying sensory neurons. Also, secretion of beta-endorphin from the anterior pituitary increases under stress, perhaps explaining the *stress-related analgesia* that sometimes occurs in soldiers with battle wounds who continue to fight in intense combat, and then later experience disabling pain in safe circumstances.

IV. NEUROTRANSMITERS, PSYCHIATRIC DISORDERS, AND PSYCHOPHARMACOLOGY

There are some well-established associations, not necessarily causal, among neurotransmitters, psychiatric disorders, and their pharmacologic treatments. However, as stated before, these associations reflect a primitive understanding of the basic pathophysiology of the disorders.

A. *Some Psychotic Disorders, Including Schizophrenia*

Neuroleptics characteristically alleviate psychotic symptoms such as delusions, hallucinations, first rank symptoms and formal thinking disorders in schizophrenia, mania, some drug-induced psychoses and some coarse brain diseases. The hypothesized main action of the neuroleptics is the blockade of dopamine receptors in the brain. From this and related data, it was postulated that dopaminergic hyperactivity was the underlying basis of schizophrenia (the *dopamine hypothesis* of *schizophrenia*).

B. *Anxiety Disorders*

Clonidine, *propranolol* (a beta-adrenergic-blocking antihypertensive, anti-migraine, and anti-tremor agent), benzodiazepines, tricyclic antidepressants, morphine and endorphins all characteristically alleviate anxiety, and all inhibit firing of the locus coeruleus. *Yohimbine*, which increases locus firing, also increases anxiety. In general, many drugs that alleviate anxiety affect catecholamine functioning. Another example of this is monoamine oxidase inhibitors, which are effective in panic disorder and agoraphobia. Benzodiazepines, barbiturates and other sedative-hypnotics, and anticonvulsants all activate GABA receptors, enhancing general neural inhibition. The new anti-anxiety drug *buspirone* acts at a subtype of 5-HT1, a serotonin receptor. But how the above associations relate to the etiology of *anxiety disorders* such as panic disorder and agoraphobia is not known.

C. *Obsessive-Compulsive Disorder*

Chlorimipramine, fluoxetine, and fluvoxamine, all anti-depressants, alleviate symptoms of *obsessive-compulsive disorder.* Among their actions, they *inhibit neuronal reuptake* of *serotonin.*

D. *Mania*

Lithium carbonate, the drug of choice for mania, inhibits both monoamine release and phosphoinositide breakdown. Interestingly, *physostigmine,* an acetylcholine agonist which is an antidote for anticholinergic delirium, transiently alleviates manic symptons, but this transiency of action renders it ineffectual as a standard treatment.

E. *Alzheimer's Disease*

In *Alzheimer's disease* (see also p. 58), a dementing disease with prominent memory problems, there are significant losses of cortical and hippocampal cholinergic axons. Also, the enzyme choline acetyl transferase, which converts choline into *acetylcholine* (which is associated with memory), is diminished by over 50% in autopsy samples of patients with Alzheimer's disease. It has been speculated that a proteinaceous factor called a *prion,* or a slow virus, acts on genetically-susceptible people to produce this dementing disorder.

F. *PCP, Mescaline, LSD and Other Hallucinogen Psychoses*

Phencyclidine (PCP, angel dust) is used as an animal tranquilizer (One would think veterinarians had better tranquilizers than this.), but as a street drug it produces anxiety, depression, suspiciousness, irritability, violence, delirium, psychosis, tachycardia, hypertension, dizziness, nystagmus and muscular incoordination. Curiously, among its actions is interference with *glutamine* (an excitatory neurotransmitter) *transmission* in the hippocampus and cortex. The hallucinogens *mescaline* and *LSD* appear to act at *5HT2,* a serotonin receptor.

G. *Endogenous Depression*

Undoubtedly, catecholamines and indoleamines are important

in depressive illness. *Reserpine*, an antihypertensive agent which depletes catecholamines, produces an endogenous depression-like syndrome. *Monoamine oxidase inhibitors* (effective in dysthymic disorder and occasionally in endogenous depression) inhibit the intracellular breakdown of catecholamines. *Tricyclic antidepressants* diminish catecholamine reuptake. *MHPG*, the principal metabolite of norepinephrine in the brain, is found in diminished quantities in the urine of endogenously depressed patients (compared to controls). The above data led to a *catecholamine hypothesis* of *depression*, but for reasons stated at the beginning of this chapter, this hypothesis is an oversimplification.

If you'd like to learn more about behavioral neurochemistry, I recommend Joseph T. Coyle's superb opening chapter in Talbott et al's 1988 *American Psychiatric Press Textbook of Psychiatry*.

V. NEUROCHEMISTRY OF CONDITIONING

Putative neurochemical mechanisms of habituation, sensitization and classic conditioning (see p. 40) were described by Kandel in studying the snail *Aplysia*. Aplysia's simple neural "wiring" begins with sensory neurons from the skin of its tail and siphon (an excretory snout). Sensory neurons synapse with motor neurons of the siphon and gill, which withdraw when the siphon is touched. *Interneurons* cross-link sensory neurons.

Habituation begins when a new sensory stimulus (e.g., touching the siphon) is presented, exciting interneurons and motor neurons, with a response such as gill withdrawal. After repeated touching of the siphon, electrical potentials in all synapses decrease, producing fewer motor action potentials in the gill. This results from *calcium channel closure* in the sensory neurons and interneurons, reducing calcium influx and diminishing neurotransmitter release.

In *sensitization*, interneurons called *facilitator interneurons* enhance neurotransmitter release by increasing *cyclic AMP* in sensory neurons. Prolonged habituation or sensitization produce visible structural neuronal changes. Aplysia's gill withdrawal can also be classically conditioned, for which the neurochemistry resembles that of sensitization.

Chapter 20:

INTERVIEWING AND PHYSICIAN-PATIENT COMMUNICATION

The goals of an initial medical interview are to obtain *data* necessary to make a diagnosis, to develop the *rapport* necessary to enhance the patient's *compliance* (see p. 17) with recommended treatments, and to begin the *inspection* and *mental status* (psychiatric) portions of the *physical examination*. Experienced physicians often develop a *differential diagnosis* (a list of the most likely diagnoses) and a *working diagnosis* (the most likely diagnosis) within the first several minutes of the interview, and in the remainder of the examination they methodically confirm or exclude their initial impressions.

The length of the initial interview varies depending on the situation. Situations range from several reassuring sentences spoken to, and several well-chosen questions asked of, a woman in shock (inadequate blood pressure and blood circulation) from gastrointestinal bleeding, while at the same time an emergency intravenous line is being inserted; to the first 20 minutes of a 40-minute office visit with an internist to establish a working diagnosis and to decide which (if any) laboratory tests to order; to an hour-long diagnostic interview in psychiatry, a specialty for which definitive laboratory tests don't yet exist.

You note the patient's age, gender, and body build; skin coloration, scars, eruptions (rashes) and decorations (e.g., tattoos, hairstyles); style and neatness of clothing; facial expressions; gait and other motor activity; cooperativeness; spontaneity and clarity of expression; presence of distress (e.g., shortwindedness, crying); and whether family members accompanied the patient. You introduce yourself, tersely explain the purpose of the interview, and (unless it is a routine employment or insurance physical) then ask a general question (e.g., "Tell me about the problem that brought you here.") to begin a *history of the present illness*. Occasionally, you cannot begin in this stereotypic fashion; for example, one of my colleagues established a fine rapport with a difficult-to-interview manic patient by the opening comment "What a lovely green dress you're wearing!"

The remainder of the history of the present illness consists of the following strategies: 1. If the patient is able to present useful information spontaneously, you can ask him *open-ended questions* such as "You said you're having lung trouble. Can you tell me more about that?" To the extent that his answer effectively guides you towards a diagnosis, continue to listen. However, you will also need to ask more specific, *closed-ended questions* (e.g., "Did anything make the cough worse?") in order to "zero-in" on crucial material. 2. When a diagnostically vital clue, in the form of an observation you have made (e.g., The patient's nose is large, red and bulbous, called a *rhinophyma* and often seen in alcoholics), or a symptom the patient has reported (e.g., the patient says "I drink a lot."), immediately or later in the interview you should question him thoroughly about other common symptoms of the condition you suspect (e.g., alcoholism). 3. Early in the interview, particularly with a psychiatric patient, it is often useful to allow the patient to speak spontaneously for several minutes (if he is able to do so), both to assess his thought processes and to convey your interest. 4. If the patient manifests *severe cognitive dysfunction* or *severe psychiatric illness* (e.g., mania with distractability), it is sometimes necessary to speak softly, ask primarily simple, closed-ended questions, and make few shifts in your body posture. You typically ask more complex and open-ended questions when interviewing a well-organized, self-controlled, thoughtful, spontaneous patient.

Later in the interview, you obtain a *past medical history, family history, personal* and *social history*, and *medical review of systems*, emphasizing data that seem most pertinent to your working and differential diagnosis. Occasionally, early in the interview, the patient presents important information that does not appear to be related to the present illness. There is usually no problem in briefly addressing this information and then returning to the present problem.

There are other techniques which *facilitate* spontaneity and rapport: 1. When it is necessary for you to change subjects, make a *transitional statement* (e.g., "I'd like to change the subject, and ask about the health of members of your family.") 2. It is sometimes useful to make *empathic comments* (Empathy means "putting yourself in the patient's position."), e.g., "I know how undignified it feels to have a barium enema," or *sympathetic comments* (Sympathy is experiencing sadness about another person's misfortune.), e.g., "I'm sorry to hear about your brother's death." 3. Occasionally, it is useful to *praise* a patient (e.g., "Doctor, I hope you're understanding me O.K." "Yes, you're explaining yourself very clearly.") However, frequent praise is rarely necessary, and this may eventually disappoint the patient if later you don't offer the praise you have led him to expect. 5. It sometimes helps to *challenge self-deprecatory statements* (e.g., "The way he treated me made me feel like a jerk." "Why should you take his insensitivity personally?"). This self-esteem-enhancing type of comment is a hallmark of *cognitive psychotherapy*.

With the exception of offering occasional praise, try to be *nonjudgmental* in initial interviews. For example, instead of asking a patient "Are you a drug addict?" "Have you ever beaten up your wife?" or "Have you ever been a pimp?" the same questions could be phrased "Did you ever do any drugs?" "Did you ever physically fight with your wife?" and "Did you ever need money so much that you had a woman work for you as a prostitute?" The objective is that the patient will not expect criticism if he answers affirmatively. However, there are times that you must be firm (e.g., "I won't prescribe a medication that I don't think will help you.") or confronting (e.g., "I can't properly evaluate and treat you if you come to the clinic intoxicated.").

Patients often ask *personal questions*, such as "Do you have experience in treating my kind of problem?" or "Are you married?" or "Are you a veteran?" If you feel a question is reasonable and appropriate, answer it briefly. However, don't let the patient "turn the interview around" by asking you a sequence of questions. One exception to this rule occurs towards the end of the initial interview, after you have summarized your findings and recommendations to the patient, and he wishes further clarification. Patients sometimes *laugh* or *joke*. If the patient says something that is funny because it is insightful, or tells a genuinely good joke (manic patients sometimes have an "infectious" sense of humor), you can laugh with him. But if the joking is cruel or self-deprecatory, you shouldn't laugh. Often, patients will *cry* or *express anger*. Usually, when the physician allows the expression of one of these emotions (and does not change subjects because of his own anxiety), the interview is enhanced. Sometimes, when the crying or anger intensify and consequently threaten to disrupt the interview, you must intervene to modify this emotion. *Unqualified reassurance* (e.g., "Don't worry. Everything will turn out fine.") should be avoided, but reassurance based on solid data (e.g., "There's an excellent chance that you'll recover from this depression," stated at the conclusion of a thorough interview.) is often helpful and necessary.

In *concluding* your initial interview, it is usually necessary to *summarize* your diagnosis and recommended treatment, as well as to answer your patient's questions, using words that he understands. Also, even if the condition you diagnose is serious and the *prognosis* (expected outcome) is poor, you should close the interview enthusiastically and hopefully. According to Dr. Elisabeth Kubler-Ross, there is always something to hope for, even if it's simply the prospect of a followup visit. The patient should not be "coldly dismissed."

Chapter 21:

FORENSIC MEDICINE

Fortunately, good medicine is usually equivalent to good law. However, compared to our predecessors, contemporary physicians must be more attentive to legal aspects of patient care (e.g., making detailed chart notes, to the point where one doctor complained that charting is, for him, like writing a legal brief). Nevertheless, physicians should cooperate with their legal colleagues, whose efforts (e.g., in lawmaking, in defense of cases) can be of inestimable value.

Doctors are expected to honor the *confidentiality* of what patients tell them. This is stated in the *Hippocratic Oath*. Maintaining privacy enhances the patient's trust and willingness to be self-revealing, consequently enhancing the physician's diagnostic and therapeutic capacity. Lawsuits can be brought against physicians for untoward consequences of revealing confidences. Nevertheless, there are multiple circumstances where legal requirements or proper care require *breach of confidentiality*; these include reporting *child abuse*, reporting certain *communicable diseases*; notifying others about *life-threatening emergencies*, e.g., notifying a family member that a suicidal patient has eloped (escaped) from the hospital; discussing a diagnostic and treatment plan with a relative of a patient when the latter is incapable of giving *informed consent* (i.e., He is legally or *de facto* incompetent.); giving *testimony in court* under subpoena when the information requested is relevant to the case; professionals in Federal hospitals reporting to the Secret Service all threats, however strange or impractical, to assassinate the President or other major Federal officials or candidates; and reporting *treason*. In cases where there is a risk of a patient harming others, the *Tarasoff case* established a precedent that the treating professional is expected to prevent this harm from occurring by appropriate care of the patient. If unable to provide such care (e.g., unable to hospitalize and treat effectively, or to convince the police to detain the patient) the physician has a *duty to warn* prospective victims. To properly address the ramifications of the Tarasoff case is beyond the scope of this book.

Doctors are required to obtain *informed consent* for examinations and treatments they prescribe. This involves providing an adequate explanation of the *indications* (reasons) for, *risks* of, and *alternatives* to the procedure, and documentation in the chart that the patient gave informed consent. Sometimes (e.g., surgical procedures), the patient must sign a detailed consent form in the presence of a "disinterested" witness, and other times (e.g., prescription of a commonly-prescribed medication) the physician may only need to note that "The indications, risks and alternatives were explained to the patient." In some hospitals, nurses quiz the patient to assess his familiarity with the medication, and record his replies in the chart.

Charting refreshes your memory about the patient's history, diagnosis and treatment, communicates with other professionals involved in the patient's care, and documents the provision of proper care. If time permits, I write chart notes as if the attorney for a potential litigant patient were sitting beside me, asking "Doctor, upon what data do you base your diagnosis, and why are you providing this treatment?"

A parent or guardian must consent to the treatment of a *minor* (usually defined as a person under 18). Exceptions are the following: (1) *Emancipated minors* are teenagers who either are married, have children, are pregnant, are self-supporting, or live independently. They may consent to medical treatment. (2) In some states, minors can receive information about, and be examined and treated for *venereal disease*. (3) In *dire emergencies*, if no parent or guardian is available, the physician can render lifesaving treatment.

Good Samaritan laws exist in all states. They hold that a doctor providing care to an adult or child patient in an emergency has *limited liability* for his actions if he doesn't crudely malpractice or abandon the patient.   *DeFINE!!!!!*

A physician may need or want to *testify in court* or in a *deposi-*

tion. A deposition is an "extension" of the court in which opposing attorneys question witnesses, and a court stenographer transcribes the testimony during the pre-trial *discovery* period. Subsequently, depositions may be read verbatim in court, without the witness needing to be present. The physician may be asked to testify as a defendant, as a witness to an occurrence, or as an *expert witness*. An expert witness, by virtue of special knowledge and experience attributed to him, may testify about his *opinions* as well as his observations.

In advance of testifying, familiarize yourself with the chart and other aspects of the case you consider important, anticipate questions you are likely to be asked (including the most sensitive, and especially those central to the case), review pertinent literature if appropriate, and ask the attorney representing "your side" whatever questions you think important. Although there are exceptions to the recommended strategies of testimony which follow, consider the following: When testifying, be sure you understand the question before you answer; think for several seconds after each question is posed instead of replying spontaneously; answer only the question posed, and do so concisely; explain the medical jargon you use without being patronizing; speak respectfully even when you feel threatened or challenged. Realize that judges, attorneys and juries are not automatically awed by your medical degree or curriculum vita. Decisions to elaborate on answers or to act righteously angry should be weighed carefully, in advance if possible, and discussed with "your side's" attorney during pre-trial discussions or recesses. Do not agree with blanket statements unless they are 100% true. Finally, it is useful to ask colleagues to be available to cover your professional responsibilities for a few days before and after the day you are expecting to testify, as court scheduling is often unpredictable.

The frequency of *lawsuits* is increasing and the cost of malpractice insurance is striking (see p. 28). Despite the attention paid to certain cases (e.g., Hinckley, Tarasoff) involving psychiatrists, of all medical specialists psychiatrists are least likely to be sued, and psychiatrists consequently pay the lowest malpractice insurance premiums.

Two arguments in favor of malpractice lawsuits are that they may deter some malpractice (For every malpractice suit there are perhaps six genuine acts of malpractice.), and that a successful suit may be the only civilized way for a victim of malpractice to obtain compensation and justice. The conventional payment for a plaintiff's attorney is the *contingent fee*, a pre-arranged percentage (usually one-third) of the money awarded. If there is no award, the plaintiff's attorney is paid minimal costs. In cases that reach court without a settlement, the physician-defendant wins 90% of the time.

The term *respondeat superior* means that employers (e.g., hospitals or physicians) and supervisors (e.g., physicians, nursing supervisors) are accountable for the professional conduct and errors of their supervisees. Furthermore, litigants' attorneys often target the *"deep-pockets,"* i.e., those most likely to be well-covered by insurance. For these reasons, as well as for good patient care, it is important for you to provide careful supervision.

A patient's *competence* may vary from situation to situation and from time to time. The key issue in competence is conformity to the applicable legal criteria, not the diagnosis per se. That a person is depressed or has diabetes does not tell the court whether he is competent. Although competence can only be determined legally in a court, physicians may be asked by the court, or seek to present to the court, their impressions of a patient's competence relative to a given situation. And in emergencies the physician must assess the patient's *de facto* (meaning "in fact" or "in essence") *competence*.

Competence for person and *competence to enter into a contract* refer to a person's ability to understand the nature and consequences of his actions in the situation at issue, such as marrying or consenting for surgery. More specialized competence-related circumstances include the following: *Testamentary capacity* is the capacity of a person to make a will, and its criteria are that the person knows 1. that he is making a will; 2. the extent and value of his possessions (his *bounty*); and 3. who are the *natural objects of his bounty* (his logical heirs, even if he chooses not to include any of them in the will). Also, there can be no duress placed upon him by any of the parties involved. *Competence to stand trial* is the ability to participate intelligently and cooperatively in one's defense. *Competence to manage funds* is the ability to use one's funds in a reasonable manner and not, because of mental illness, grossly hoard or squander them. In the V.A. system, a physician's impression of the patient's competence to manage V.A. disability monies usually suffices, without relying on a court hearing, regarding the patient's receipt of V.A. disability benefits.

All states have statutes that a person can be *hospitalized involuntarily* if, as a product of a mental illness, there is *"clear* and *convincing"* evidence of *dangerousness*, i.e., that in the near future he may kill or maim himself or others or be unable to care for himself or solicit others to care for him. In a few states, a risk of massive damage to property can also justify involuntary hospitalization. Legal theorists consider "clear and convincing" a less demanding standard than the *"beyond a reasonable doubt"* criterion in criminal trials. Legal and ethical justifications for involuntary hospitalization are *parens patriae* (the duty of the state to protect a person from himself if he cannot act in his own best interests) and the state's *police power* (its duty to protect others from a dangerous individual). A psychiatrist or other physician or mental health professional may involuntarily admit a dangerous patient for several days of observation and treatment without a court order. Beyond this initial period, if the patient continues to be dangerous and to reject hospitalization, extended involuntary hospitalization requires a *commitment* hearing before a judge (and a jury if the patient wishes) in which the patient has the right to an attorney, the right to cross-examine, the right not to testify against himself, the right to call witnesses in his behalf, a right to appeal the decision, and the right to followup review of his status.

Several *right-to-treatment* court decisions established a precedent that a person committed to a public psychiatric facility was entitled to a quality of care well beyond custodial observation in a locked facility. Several *right-to-refuse treatment* court decisions established a precedent in many states that a committed patient presumed to be competent could refuse "extraordinary" treatments, which in some states include even ECT and neuroleptic drugs (In "my book," these are not "extraordinary" treatments.). For such treatments to be used, these states require deliberation by a designated independent third party, e.g., a psychiatrist, a panel of professionals and lay people, or a court. In the latter case, long delays often arise before the court hears the case. During the pre-hearing waiting period, effective treatment often cannot be prescribed, and there is evidence that a significant number of untoward consequences to patients and staff have resulted.

In the case of patients committed as dangerous to others, and then treated and discharged as improved, several states mandate *outpatient commitment* whereby the patient is required to receive specific followup treatment. Initial reports from these states raise doubts about the efficacy of these statutes.

Chapter 22:

MEDICAL ETHICS

Medical ethics is a new discipline which has interfaces with medicine, philosophy and law. Although ethics in medicine has received attention for centuries, dramatic developments (e.g., DNA recombination techniques) and controversial, publicized cases (e.g., the Baby Doe case) during the past three decades suggested that a new discipline focus on moral dilemmas in medical care.

The *physician's responsibility to his patient* is to diagnose the patient's condition, and to educate him about its signs, symptoms, treatments and prognosis. Taking the patient's wishes and life circumstances into account, he is expected to implement and monitor his treatment recommendations. Sometimes, other factors impinge upon fulfillment of these obligations. For example, a patient incompetent "for person" typically cannot be meaningfully educated about his illness.

The ethical medical conduct of a case is influenced by *priorities* (e.g., great weight must be given to the wishes of a well-informed, competent person.), *principles* (e.g., the principle of *nonmaleficence,* the classic Latin expression for which is "*Primum non nocere,*" meaning "First, do no harm" to your patient.), *philosophical perspectives* (e.g., the perspective that withholding life-sustaining medical treatment from an infant with multiple profound deformities, but with the potential for years of survival, is wrong regardless of the costs to society), and *situations* (e.g., court hearings to determine a patient's competence and to

116

appoint a guardian can rarely be convened fast enough in medical emergencies).

Jonsen, Siegler and Winslade, in their thoughtful, practical text *Clinical Ethics*, recommend that for physicians to accomplish their goals in serving their patients and society, there should be an order of ethical priorities that applies to most cases, but which permits or obligates rearrangement in some cases. The order is 1. *patient preferences*; 2. *medical indications*; 3. *quality of life*; and 4. *external factors*.

The patient preference priority is based on the principle of *autonomy*, articulated by John Stuart Mill in 1859: "Over himself, his own body and mind, the individual is sovereign." Examples of application of this priority include the following: 1. A competent, nondangerous person can terminate the doctor-patient relationship at any time. 2. Thirty-eight states recognize a *living will*, a standardized document signed by the patient stating that if he becomes unable to make decisions while comatose, he does not want his life artificially prolonged if there is virtually no hope of his regaining the ability to reason and to experience pleasure. 3. An adult practicing *Jehovah's Witness* may and will refuse transfusions of others' blood. For elective surgery some Witnesses will accept *autotransfusion* (the storage and consequent transfusion of one's own blood). An adult practicing *Christian Scientist* will not and need not seek medical care for a curable, life-threatening disease. Fascinatingly, some insurance companies offer life insurance to Christian Scientists, and some (including Blue Cross/Blue Shield) insure Christian Scientists for treatment by prayer in a Christian Science sanitarium.

But there are circumstances in which autonomy is limited. For example, a patient cannot compel a physician to prescribe a treatment that the latter feels to be useless, inadequate or dangerous. Guardians make medical decisions for patients who are legally incompetent for person. Although adult Jehovah's Witnesses may refuse transfusions, courts have ordered transfusions for minor children of Witnesses, because "Parents may make martyrs of themselves, but they are not free to make martyrs of their children."

Second on the Jonsen priority list is *medical indications,* which are fulfilled as discussed on page 116 in the paragraph on the doctor's responsibility to the patient. Buttressing the priority of the doctor's providing appropriate medical care are the principles of *beneficence* and nonmaleficence (see page 116). According to Beauchamp and Childress, beneficence is a *duty*, distinct from mercy, kindness and charity, "to help others further their legitimate interests . . . that requires the provision of benefits and the prevention and removal of harm."

Good Samaritan laws (see p. 112) foster beneficence in emergencies. Additional rationales for acting beneficently in emergencies are *implied consent* and *therapeutic privilege*. Neither implied consent nor therapeutic privilege is based upon legislation or decisive court decisions, but a physician could invoke either of them. When a patient is (legally or de facto) incompetent to consent to a life-saving emergency procedure, and there is no time to spare, the physician could proceed on the basis of *implied consent,* a theoretical presumption that the patient would consent if he were competent.

If there are only several hours' leeway and the patient is legally incompetent, the patient's guardian could consent to the patient's care. If the patient is de facto incompetent, a second opinion from a colleague, and discussions with the hospital department chief, a hospital administrator, and one or more relatives could be helpful. The relatives are the most likely to represent what would be the patient's wishes, as well as the most likely to sue if they are not consulted and the patient dies. But despite the importance of the relatives' support, a relative's proxy consent is not binding in most states unless the relative has been declared by a court to be the guardian.

If days or weeks are available, making the situation non-emergent, a court should be petitioned to declare the patient incompetent for person and appoint a guardian to make decisions for the patient. Sometimes there are long delays awaiting a competency hearing, and no family member or friend is willing or able to serve as guardian. Innovative approaches to this problem have included (in two counties in New York State) multidisciplinary *volunteer committees* serving as surrogates for judges, and psychiatrists not previously involved in a psychiatric patient's care serving as guardians.

Therapeutic privilege can justify not providing full information to a patient prior to prescribing emergency treatment in certain situations. For example, it is unwise to inform a combative, psychotic patient about the side effects of neuroleptic drugs just before giving him an emergency intramuscular injection of haloperidol. And some patients with severe ventricular irritability could die during a weighty discussion of treatment risks. As therapeutic privilege is the exception, not the rule, its invocation must be justified in the chart.

Regarding *nonmaleficence,* the following apply: Don't lie to a patient. This risks losing the patient's trust if the lie is detected. For the same reason, don't prescribe *placebos* (inert substances disguised as medications) except in research with the patient's informed consent. The doctor may not administer a *lethal injection,* even to a terminally ill patient who is comatose or suffering intensely. Remember, Nazi Germany's "euthanasia" program began with the terminally ill. The law also forbids assisting in a *suicide,* and well it should: Many terminally ill, depressed, suicidal individuals can be treated successfully for depression.

Third on the Jonsen priority list is *quality of life.* This is an ambiguous, relative concept. What I consider a meaningful life may be different from one that you consider to be worth living. Based upon the priority of autonomy, it is the patient (presumed to be competent until there is evidence to the contrary) who decided whether his life is worth living. A mentally retarded, quadriplegic, terminally ill, AIDS-victimized, unemployed, or impoverished person may view his existence affirmatively.

However, as of 1988 there is some consensus in professional and lay communities that the quality of a patient's life falls below a minimum threshold when he has a terminal illness, (e.g., extensive metastatic cancer, advanced amyotrophic lateral sclerosis), his life is sustained in a vegetative state, there is no realistic hope of recovery from this state, his preferences are unknown (or he is known, as by a living will, to have opposed maintenance of a vegetative existence), and his family and staff disapprove of maintaining his life by respirators, intravenous lines, and other medical devices, or performing cardiopulmonary resuscitation. In such cases, physicians may withhold or remove life supports. Court decisions have supported this course of action. However, Jonsen recommends that hospitals maintain ethics committees to address such cases as they occur, and that hospital attorneys prepare guidelines for professional staffs to conform to local law.

It is often recommended that for a competent patient whose advanced age, chronic illness or terminal illness puts him at risk for cardiac arrest or a permanent vegetative state, the latter two possibilities should be tactfully discussed with him and his family early in the course of his care, at such time as he appears receptive to such a discussion. Then, if the patient wishes, *do not resuscitate* orders may be written, and noted on the outside of his chart.

The final item on the Jonsen list is other (miscellaneous) considerations. These include costs of, and access to, medical care; family considerations; teaching; and research. A country's health care system strongly influences who will receive what care and how promptly. In the *British system,* all citizens are entitled to free health care funded by taxes. However, because health care resources are limited, not all procedures are promptly available; for example, it may take years on a waiting list to obtain a hip replacement.

Family considerations have been discussed elsewhere. Also note that family members cannot be compelled to donate an organ to a relative, even if the latter dies as a result of the refusal. *Organ donation* must be a freely-granted, generous gift.

Although most patients graciously consent to be *teaching subjects,* and many consent to being *research subjects,* they must give informed consent in both of these roles. Refusals should be accepted respectfully.

Medical ethics has rapidly acquired, and developed a foundation upon, a roster of famous cases, including the following: 1. In 1973, in *Roe vs. Wade,* the U.S. Supreme Court ruled that a woman has the right to an abortion. During the first *trimester* (three calendar months) of pregnancy, the state can place no limitations on the procedure, respecting the woman's autonomous *right-to-privacy.* The decision is hers, to be made in concert with the judgment of her physician that the procedure is indicated. During the second trimester, the state's interest is ambiguous. During the third trimester, when the fetus is usually *viable* (able to survive outside the womb), a state, using its police powers to protect the lives of the viable fetus, may forbid abortion except when used to save the mother's life.

2. In their 1989 *Webster vs Reproductive Health Services* ruling, a conservative Supreme Court would not overrule Roe vs. Wade, but gave each state the right to place further restrictions on abortion. This has led to unusually intense political debate in every state, affecting the outcome of every 1989 political campaign.

3. The *Baby Doe* case resulted in a 1984 amendment to the Child Abuse Prevention Act and a 1986 Supreme Court decision, both of which took the *deontologic* position (a position that certain acts are absolutely wrong—or right—regardless of the consequences) that the termination of life-sustaining medical

treatment (e.g., cardiac catheterization and subsequent cardiac surgery) to a profoundly handicapped newborn (with the potential for years of life) is child abuse. Withholding treatment except for medication, nutrition and hydration is, however, acceptable if the infant is irreversibly comatose or with virtually no chance of survival. A sizeable proportion of neonatologists (pediatricians for newborns) privately take the *utilitarian* position (that of the late British philosopher Jeremy Bentham) who stated that the main goal of a society is the "greatest good for the greatest number") that excessive resources are devoted to these newborns, depriving larger numbers of healthier infants of valuable resources.

GLOSSARY

Acquired Immune Deficiency Syndrome (AIDS): a fatal syndrome in which a virus attacks immunity-helping lymphocytes, leaving the patient susceptible to a variety of infections rarely seen in patients with normal immunity. In the U.S., it is more frequent among gays, intravenous drug abusers and people requiring frequent blood transfusions. There is a high frequency of severe secondary behavioral abnormalities.

Alcoholism: a common, serious, recurrent disorder. Full-blown, it is characterized by medical complications (e.g., withdrawal shaking and loss of memory—called "blackouts"—for periods of time when one was intoxicated); typical habits (e.g., drinking before breakfast); social complications (such as marital problems or arrests for driving while intoxicated); and the perception by the patient, friends or relatives that he has a drinking problem.

Amphetamines: a group of stimulant drugs (e.g., dextroamphetamine) with sympathomimetic properties such as increased pulse and blood pressure. They are useful in the treatment of minimal brain dysfunction/hyperactivity syndrome. However, they are often abused as street drugs.

Anorexia nervosa: a condition seen most often in teenage girls who incorrectly believe that they are overweight and must diet stringently to lose weight. They usually lose over 25% of their original weight and experience complications of starvation, and 9% die.

Barbiturates: a group of sedative-hypnotic and anticonvulsant drugs (e.g., amobarbital/Amytal and phenobarbital). They can be addicting if prescribed improperly or abused as street drugs.

Benzodiazepines: a group of anti-anxiety, sedative-hypnotic and anticonvulsant drugs such as diazepam (Valium), chlordiazepoxide (Librium), and flurazepam (Dalmane). To a lesser extent than for barbiturates, they can be addicting if prescribed improperly or abused as street drugs.

Bipolar disorder: a common and usually severe <u>mood disorder</u> defined by the experience of one or more episodes of mania (see mania), regardless of whether the patient also has episodes of endogenous depression (see depression, endogenous) to which he is predisposed.

Briquet's syndrome: a condition characterized by numerous medically-unexplained symptoms, starting before age 30 and often leading to unnecessary hospitalizations and surgery.

Carbamazepine (Tegretol): an anticonvulsant and anti-manic agent with particular usefulness in the treatment of psychomotor epilepsy.

Coarse brain disease: synonymous with the term organic brain disease, this is a group of brain disorders among whose signs are abnormal behaviors. When coarse disease is present, physical or laboratory examinations usually show clear-cut positive findings (e.g., paralysis of one side of the body, mass in the brain visible on computerized tomographic brain scan, extremely low levels of blood sugar) and (unlike most psychiatric syndromes) often have a known cause (e.g., blood clot or tumor in the brain, diabetes).

Cognitive functioning: intellectual functioning. It refers to behaviors (e.g., solving math problems, writing) reflecting functions of the secondary and tertiary cortex ("higher centers") of the brain.

Conversion disorder: a "pseudoneurologic" syndrome in which the findings are not consistent with known pathophysiology (e.g., "paralysis" of a limb with normal reflexes and no classic pathologic reflexes). Many conversion disorders are not conversion disorders at all, turning out to be manifestations of clear-cut neurologic disease (e.g., multiple sclerosis) or psychiatric illness (e.g., Briquet's syndrome).

Delirium tremens: a life-threatening condition caused by withdrawal from alcohol or certain sedative-hypnotics (e.g., barbiturates, benzodiazepines). Classic manifestations include trembling of the hands, extensive cognitive dysfunction, changing levels of consciousness, hallucinations, illusions and muttering.

Delusions: Fixed (un-shakeable) false beliefs (e.g., "I am President Reagan, President Eisenhower and President Cleveland.") which are not held by the patient's friends, relatives, colleagues, or members of his religion or ethnic group.

Dementia: a group of conditions characterized by extensive cognitive dysfunction in the presence of a normal level of consciousness. Modern neurologists and psychiatrists no longer define dementia as leading to deterioration. A number of curable conditions (e.g., folic acid deficiency, hypothyroidism, endogenous depression) are referred to as "treatable dementias."

Depression: a group of disorders of mood, beyond normal reactive sadness, characterized by findings like sadness, pessimism, appetite disturbances and trouble sleeping.

Depression, endogenous: this is synonymous with "major depressive episode with melancholia," and "bipolar disorder, depressed phase." It is a common type of depression associated with a high frequency of suicide. It is characterized by a sustained sad or anxious mood, appetite and weight loss, trouble staying asleep, agitated or slowed-down motor behavior, significant feelings of guilt, worthlessness or hopelessness, and a tendency for the mood to be worse in the morning and improve slightly as the day progresses.

Dexamethasone suppression test (D.S.T.): borrowed from internal medicine, the D.S.T. is performed by administering 1 mg. of dexamethasone (a synthetic corticosteroid hormone) to the patient at 11:30 p.m. and obtaining plasma cortisol levels at 4 p.m. and 11 p.m. the following day. A cortisol level at either time greater than 5 mcg./dl. is defined as abnormal and is 96% specific and 43% sensitive in diagnosing endogenous depression in psychiatric inpatients.

DSMIIIR: The Diagnostic and Statistical Manual of the American Psychiatric Association, Third Edition, Revised Version. The "official" listing of the criteria needed for the diagnoses of psychiatric syndromes. Its precursor, DSMIII, was the first diagnostic manual to strive for good inter-rater reliability (see p. 12), using the strategy of requiring clearly specified (*operationalized*) criteria for making diagnoses. Unfortunately, not all conditions listed in DSMIII or DSMIIIR are well-validated, discrete disorders with common family patterns, laboratory characterizations, responses to treatment, or outcomes (prognoses). Although generally accepted by psychiatrists because of its operationalized, atheoretical approach, few psychiatrists have committed DSMIII criteria to memory, or used these criteria "religiously," and this may also be the case for DSM-IIIR.

Epilepsy: a paroxysmal (having a tendency to spasms or convulsions of sudden onset), transitory (temporary), disturbance of brain functioning which usually starts suddenly, stops spontaneously and recurs.

Hallucinations: perceptions for which there is no external stimulus. Hallucinations can be seen in countless psychiatric and general medical disorders, as well as in 50% of normals (at some time in their lives). Examples include smelling a foul order when there is no such odor (especially associated with temporal lobe psychomotor epilepsy), seeing animals when no animals are present (stereotypically associated with delirium tremens), and hearing vivid conversations about oneself when one is alone (frequent in schizophrenia, mania and endogenous depression).

Hypertension: high blood pressure, which when sustained or severe can lead to heart failure or cerebral vascular accidents (strokes).

Hypochondriasis: preoccupation with one's symptoms, signs and illnesses. It is seen in many conditions, including Briquet's syndrome and endogenous depression.

Illusions: misperceptions of real external stimuli. Normal examples include the images in amusement park fun-house mirrors and the stage performances of magicians. Pathologic examples include the changes in size and shape of objects experienced in temporal lobe psychomotor epilepsy, or the wavering of walls experienced by some patients intoxicated with lysergic acid diethylamide (LSD).

Imipramine (Tofranil): a tricyclic antidepressant drug, it is used in the treatment of endogenous depression and panic disorder.

Influenza: a group of viral disorders caused by several different influenza viruses. Depending upon host-virus factors, influenzas range in severity from mild to fatal.

Lithium: prescribed as lithium carbonate tablets or lithium citrate syrup, it is a salt found in the earth's crust. Its primary uses are the treatment of mania and the prevention of mania in patients with previous manic or endogenous depressed episodes.

Meprobamate: an anti-anxiety drug of the propylenediol class, its use is in disfavor because of its high addiction potential.

Minimum brain dysfunction/hyperactivity syndrome: this common cause of referral to child psychiatry clinics is characterized by an inability to focus attention for prolonged periods of time (the child responds too readily to distractions), learning difficulties, and mild nonspecific neurologic and electroencephalographic findings.

Monoamine Oxidase Inhibitors (MAOIs): a group of drugs (e.g., phenelzine/Nardil) that inactivates the enzyme monoamine oxidase (MAO). Because MAO breaks down catecholamines such as norepinephrine, use of MAOIs causes increased brain catecholamine levels. MAOIs are used in the treatment of panic disorder, phobias secondary to panic disorder, and atypical depressions.

Myocardial infarction: death of heart muscle tissue due to inadequate coronary arterial blood supply, usually secondary to lipid deposits occluding the lumen of coronary arteries. A common cause of fatal "heart attack."

Narcolepsy: a condition characterized by a tendency to enter REM sleep either at the beginning of the sleep cycle (causing hypnogogic hallucinations, meaning hallucinations upon falling asleep), randomly during the day (causing sleep attacks at inopportune times), or with strong emotion or exertion (leading to muscle weakness or falling, called cataplexy).

Neuroleptic drugs: a group of drugs that includes these subgroups: phenothiazines (e.g., chlorpromazine/Thorazine), butyrophenones (e.g., haloperidol/Haldol), dihydroindolones (e.g., molindone/Moban), thioxanthines (e.g., thiothixene/Navane), and dibenzoxazepines (e.g., loxapine/Loxitane). They are used in the acute treatment of certain psychotic disorders and in the extended (up to a year at a time) treatment of schizophrenia.

Neurosis: defined as a condition caused by an unconscious conflict. Examples include panic disorder, phobias, and obsessive-compulsive disorder.

Obsessive-compulsive disorder: a condition characterized by frequent unwanted, intrusive thoughts (obsessions, e.g., "I keep thinking I'm dirty, which is untrue and ridiculous, no matter how much I wash.") which the patient knows are absurd but can't dismiss, and frequent impractical, unnecessary actions (compulsions, e.g., repetitive hand-washing) in response to the obsessions.

Phenothiazines: a subgroup of neuroleptic drugs.

Posttraumatic stress disorder (PTSD): a condition precipitated by exposure to a noxious event (e.g., being raped, being in combat) far in excess of that experienced in the ordinary course of life. Symptoms include frequent re-experiencing of the event as memories or nightmares, feeling alienated from others, and having sleep difficulty or survivor guilt. Most PTSD patients have co-existing psychiatric disorders.

Projection: a defense mechanism whereby one unconsciously attributes one's unwanted impulses (e.g., to kill one's boss) to another person (e.g., "My boss wants to kill me").

Propylenediols: a group of anti-anxiety drugs (including meprobamate) currently in disfavor because of high addiction potential.

Psychosis: craziness. An imprecise term for any psychiatric condition rendering the patient unable to perform life's ordinary tasks because of severe cognitive dysfunction, delusions or hallucinations.

REM sleep: rapid eye movement sleep, which occurs every 90–110 minutes during sleep. Associated with increased heart rate and blood pressure, rapid and deep breathing, decreased muscle tone in most muscles, and vivid, recallable dreams.

Schizophrenia: a much-overdiagnosed condition which when rigorously diagnosed affects 5% of psychiatrically-hospitalized patients. It is chronic and leads to progressive disability.

Sociopathy: A lifelong condition characterized by impaired performance in multiple facets of life due to selfishness, impulsivity and callousness. Common behaviors of adult sociopaths include arrests, fights, abandonment of family, firings from jobs, and habitual lying. Synonymous with antisocial personality disorder.

Superego: conscience

Tardive dyskinesia: Choreoathetoid movements (see p. 44) of the mouth, face, extremities or trunk resulting from long-term (months to years) use of neuroleptic drugs. As it is, to date, incurable (except occasionally when mild signs are identified early in treatment and the neuroleptic is discontinued), the physician is obligated to inform the patient about this long-term risk if ongoing neuroleptic treatment is indicated, and to document that the patient was informed of the risk.

Tricyclic antidepressants: a group of drugs (e.g., imipramine/Tofranil and amitryptiline/Elavil) whose main indication is endogenous depression. Also used in the treatment of panic disorder, posttraumatic stress disorder, and chronic pain syndromes.

Tuberculosis: an infection by the tubercle bacillus that used to be very common and was often fatal. Now it is rarely fatal if diagnosed and treated properly, and is common only among alcoholics and poor people living in overcrowded conditions. It can cause disease in most organs, but most frequently infects the lungs.

INDEX

RAPID LEARNING AND RETENTION
THROUGH THE MEDMASTER SERIES:

CLINICAL NEUROANATOMY MADE RIDICULOUSLY SIMPLE, by S. Goldberg, M.D. (1989); 87 pgs., 61 illustr.; (Spanish translation, at same price); $10.95.

CLINICAL ANATOMY MADE RIDICULOUSLY SIMPLE, by S. Goldberg, M.D. (1987). A systemic approach to clinical anatomy utilizing a high picture-to-text ratio. Memory is facilitated by conceptual diagrams, ridiculous associations, and a strong focus on clinical relevance. Excellent Board review; 175 pgs., 303 illustr.; $16.95.

OPHTHALMOLOGY MADE RIDICULOUSLY SIMPLE, by S. Goldberg, M.D. (1988). All the ophthalmology necessary for the non-ophthalmologist; 82 pgs., 75 illustr.; $10.95.

PSYCHIATRY MADE RIDICULOUSLY SIMPLE, by W.V. Good, M.D. and J. Nelson, M.D. (1987). A delightful and practical guide to clinical psychiatry; 85 pgs., 20 illustr.; $10.95.

ACUTE RENAL INSUFFICIENCY MADE RIDICULOUSLY SIMPLE, by C. Rotellar, M.D. (1988). A brief, clear, practical, and humorous approach to acute renal insufficiency; 56 pgs., 49 illustr.; $8.95.

THE FOUR-MINUTE NEUROLOGIC EXAM, by S. Goldberg, M.D. (1988). A guide to rapid neurologic assessment, when time is limited; 58 pgs., 13 illustr.; $8.95.

CLINICAL ANATOMY AND PATHOPHYSIOLOGY FOR THE HEALTH PROFESSIONAL, by J.V. Stewart, M.D. (1989). For nursing students and other health professionals. Brief, clear, strong clinical focus; 260 pgs., 230 illustr.; $16.95.

BEHAVIORAL SCIENCE FOR THE BOREDS, by F.S. Sierles, M.D. (1989). A concise review of the Behavioral Sciences for Part I of the National Boards; (2nd Edition) 127 pgs.; $12.95.

CLINICAL BIOCHEMISTRY MADE RIDICULOUSLY SIMPLE, by S. Goldberg, M.D. (1988). A conceptual approach to clinical biochemistry, with humor. Includes a color map of Biochemistryland (an amusement park in which clinical biochemistry is seen as a whole, along with its key pathways, diseases, drugs, and laboratory tests). For biochemistry courses and medical Board review. hardcover. 95 pgs.; $20.95

JONAH: THE ANATOMY OF THE SOUL, by S. Goldberg, M.D. (1989). A new appraisal of the mind-body problem and its relations to quantum physics. Presents the strongest case to date for the presence of consciousness in computers and the persistence of the conscious mind after death; 95 pgs.; $8.95.

CLINICAL PSYCHOPHARMACOLOGY MADE RIDICULOUSLY SIMPLE, by J. Preston, Psy. D. and J. Johnson, M.D. (1990). A brief, practical review of the indications for and use of pharmacologic agents in the treatment of psychologic disorders. 42 pgs.; $8.95.

Try your bookstore for these, or, if unavailable, send the above amounts (plus $2.00 postage and handling per total order) to:

MedMaster, Inc.   P.O. Box 640028   Dept. BBK   Miami, FL 33164

Obsessive Compulsive — Mania
- Reax/formation   Reax/formation
- Doing & Undoing
- Intellectualization
- Isolation

Paranoid conditions
- Projection